YOUR LIFE, DESIGNED

**Practical Feng Shui
Advice to Assist You in
Creating Your Life
From the Outside In**

By

Leigh Kubin

**Fame's Eternal Books, LLC
United States of America**

Copyright © 2007 by Leigh Kubin
Cover art by Kat Graham
www.katgraham.com

ISBN: 978-0-9753721-7-3

All rights reserved. No part of this book may be reproduced or transmitted in any form by any means, electronic or mechanical, including photocopying, recording, or by any information storage and retrieval system, without written permission of the author, except for the inclusion of brief quotations in reviews.

Printed in the United States of America

For additional information, contact:

Fame's Eternal Books, LLC at

TammyMate@aol.com or
1-512-468-8873

Contents

Preface _____ *ix*

Foreword _____ *xi*

Chapter 1 What Is Feng Shui ?_____ 2
Chapter 2 What Is Your Element_____ 12
Chapter 3 The Ba Gua _____ 44
Chapter 4 What Are You Going Create?
(Your Three Objectives)_____ 72
Chapter 5 The Center _____ 88
Chapter 6 The Journey_____ 96
Chapter 7 Self-Knowledge_____ 106
Chapter 8 Ancestry_____ 112
Chapter 9 Abundance_____ 122
Chapter 10 Fame / Reputation_____ 130
Chapter 11 Relationships_____ 138
Chapter 12 Creativity / Children_____ 148
Chapter 13 Helpful People / Travel_____ 154
Chapter 14 Limiting Beliefs and Balance_____ 160

*Conclusion*_____ 170

Appendix A Interesting Stories_____ 174

Appendix B Q & A with Leigh & Paul_____ 182

Dedication

To my family, you inspire me by reminding me every day that anything is possible, that we get to be anything we want and to never give up. Thank you for sharing this journey with me, I Love You!

Preface

The purpose of this book is to show those who are interested, the benefits of using Feng Shui. This is not the only way to create harmony and balance in your home; however, it is the way we have created it in ours. It is simply a fun form of therapy. If you choose to go deep inside and look, you will transform your life. We do not say that if you don't use Feng Shui, you will have horrible things happen to you. This is just a way to adjust your life according to what you are trying to create.

You create everything about your life, and attract every situation to you. There is a way to consciously choose what you want your life to look and feel like. Sometimes things show up and we say, I didn't order that. Well the universe thought you did, so on some level, you did! Enjoy it, there are no mistakes here; only opportunities to learn and grow.

I will explain what each section of the BaGua means to you personally and ways to use this knowledge to create specific things in your life. I am using stories from our business, and our personal life; the do's and don'ts. There are many things that you can do for yourself using Feng Shui. However, to get deep, I strongly recommend our on-line course that goes along with this book (or a certified practitioner.) You will have many answers at your fingertips that you don't get with other books.

Our web address is:
www.thefengshuitrainingcenter.com
Our Feng Shui forum can be found at
www.thefengshuitrainingcenter.com/studentlounge

Foreward

I have chosen to place *chi flow* in the beginning so that you can read through it first and then refer back to it as you begin to work in each sector. Understanding chi flow is vital for your adjustments! If you have clutter, clear it out now. It blocks the flow of energy through your home and creates stagnation. No excuses! If you really want change, you need to get rid of it!

"Joy is the feeling associated with freely circulating energy. Pain is the feeling associated with a block or interruption in the free flow of energy." (*Taoist Teaching, We Are One*. Lawrence Boldt)

Feng Shui is based on the awareness that electromagnetic energy (known as *chi*) flows around and through your body, linking you to every other person, object and force in the universe. This vibrating energy field is the literal manifestation of the Taoist teaching that "We are all one." You can feel this energetic connection to others when you know that someone is behind you without turning around. Or perhaps you've walked into a room where two people have been arguing. Even if the room is now silent, the energetic imprint of the prior emotions remains affecting the energy in the room.

Chi moves and changes form constantly. The chi in your body can transfer to the external environment and vice versa. Think of the last time you sat down in a leather chair on a cold winter day. You transferred quite a bit of energy to that chair to warm it up before it gave anything back in the form of comfort.

The Chinese believe that there are two guiding principles in working with chi:

1. Everything is constantly changing.
2. The changes are predictable.

Based on this belief, Chinese scholars created the text known as the I Ching (Book of Changes). The I Ching was their map for predicting change in social systems. When Feng Shui developed, the scholars used a variation of the I Ching, known as the Ba Gua map, to predict change in environmental systems. In addition to the Ba Gua map, the entire body of Feng Shui knowledge is built around understanding how to:

- Attract chi
- Disperse chi
- Balance the chi of the environment with the chi of the individual
- Predict energetic shifts
- Modify energetic shifts to produce desirable outcomes

Feng Shui is based on the principle that chi patterns are predictable. Once we understand how energy flows, both within our bodies and between our bodies and the environment, we can create environments that sustain the energy patterns we want to have.

Instead of focusing solely on how our inner beliefs change our outer experiences, Feng Shui teaches that our outer environment can also affect changes in our inner reality. In this age of self-help, the environmental approach is often overlooked. The objects and energy with which we surround ourselves on a daily basis send a message about who we are, what we can attain, what our limitations are, whether or not we are lovable, and so forth. Denise Linn writes that the beliefs in your energy field "act as magnets, pulling to you situations and people that are congruous with your subconscious beliefs." An example of this phenomenon is people who feel that they can't trust anyone. This belief is being constantly projected in their energy field, even when they're feeling relatively calm and trusting. The vibrations from their energy field act as a magnet, drawing people to them who truly act in untrustworthy ways.

Changing your external surroundings, and thereby changing the daily messages that you send yourself and the rest of the world, changes your inner reality.

Chi Flow Factors (Chi in the Home):

- Doors
- Windows
- Lighting
- Furniture items

- Plants
- Color
- Number of animals and people in the space
- Shape of rooms (corners, wall projections, curved walls)

Tracking Chi Flow Through A Room

Before you can adjust chi flow patterns, you need to identify what the current patterns are. The following list is key, not only in tracking chi flow, but in adjusting it as well. The goal is to attract chi, allow it to circulate in an area, and allow it to move on again:

- **Locate the primary door.** This is the mouth of chi for that room and the main source of energy. The chi will flow from this door into the room.

- **Look for doors or windows directly opposite the primary door.** If there is a door or a window opposite the main door, the chi will flow directly through the room and out the other side.

- **Look for secondary doors or windows.** Even when doors or windows are not directly opposite the main door, they will attract chi and the flow will move from the main door around and out the other doors and windows. Secondary doors and windows help the chi circulate before it leaves the room.

- **Identify patterns of circulation.** What in the room encourages the chi to move? You can help move the chi using walls, furniture, lighting, plants, and other Feng Shui adjustment items.

- **Look for possible bottlenecks.** Areas that are too narrow push the chi. If these narrow areas are long, such as a long narrow hallway, the chi will speed up and move too quickly to be comfortable for human beings. Other bottlenecks can occur when too many doors open into the same area. If doors are misaligned, this creates fighting doors.

- **Locate possible stagnation.** Are there places where the chi will slow too much? Corners, dark areas, rooms with too much furniture, and items low to the ground can all trap chi and create stagnation.

- **Locate stairs.** Stairs will move chi quickly up and down. This chi is often volatile and needs to be softened through the use of filled risers, carpet, plants, crystals, wall art, or other balancing items.

Resisting Chi Flow

When we resist and impede the flow of chi through our bodies and through our lives, we experience the following:

- Holding onto our breath, which impedes the circulation of oxygen and produces pain.
- Holding our muscles in place (chronic tension), which impedes circulation and produces pain.
- Holding onto limiting beliefs, which impedes mental circulation and produces pain.
- Holding onto grudges or resentments, which impedes the circulation of emotional energy and produces pain.
- Withholding expression of our natural gifts, which impedes circulation and produces pain.

Resistance In The Home

Resisting chi is evident in the home environment through blockages of all sorts. Blocked doors and windows are the most common. However a piece of furniture can block passage through a room, and a small entrance hall can create a blocked feeling the minute you walk in.

To Support You In Clearing Out Resistance:

- Open the physical/energetic center of the home by hanging a 40mm round faceted crystal.

- Open up the center of individual rooms by moving furniture, or adding a light fixture.

- Unblock doors on the inside.

- Use mirrors to move chi through any exterior items that may be blocking the front door.

- Clear away overgrown plants and trees that may be blocking windows.

- Clean windows.

- Make certain that windows can open, allowing chi to pass in and through the home.

- Make certain window coverings can be pulled back easily and that cording works.

- Clutter clear any stacks or boxes.

- Get heavy items off the floor.

- Clean out and sweep corners.

- Space clear the home.

- Open windows and doors, allowing air to pass through the home.

- Use colors that are clear and have "flow." (No muted or grayed earth tones.)

- Bring more light (natural or not) into the home. Consider skylights, lamps, installed fixtures, sheer window treatments, new windows, mirrors, and reflective surfaces.

Chapter 1
What Is Feng Shui?

The term Feng Shui actually means wind & water. But what does that term really mean? Let's look at a few things that will clarify this so that you can answer that question for yourself. What would your ideal place to live look like? My ideal place is more a state of mind than an actual "place." We can actually create our ideal place with our words and thoughts. The ideal place for me is a place that encourages me and my family to grow, to think outside the box, to reach our potential--fearlessly. I feel the beauty of this every day, knowing that I am in my ideal place when I see my husband and our children following their dreams. I know that we are in the ideal place, and I rarely forget to ask, "How does it get any better than this?" One thing I have noticed about living in our ideal place is that I never hear any of us say, "Oh, I can't do this!" Instead, it is always phrased "What do I need to do to create this?"

What we think about most is what we experience most. When we focus on the beauty and goodness around us, we begin to notice more beauty and goodness. When we focus on fear or lack, this is what we experience. The saying, "The rich get richer and the poor get poorer," is so true. The reason this is true is because of the thoughts of the people. The ones thinking, "I have more than enough" are open to more. The ones thinking, "I don't have enough" aren't focused on more. They are focused on lack. So, they experience lack. We get what we focus on. The beautiful thing I have found with this "law of attraction" (*The Secret*, 2005) is that I can decide what I would like to create in my life, visualize it; and it materializes! If something shows up that isn't what I want, I just change my thinking about it. Creating our ideal place does require action. We can't just sit back and wait for things to happen. We must act. "When the inspired ideas come, we trust it." (Joe Vitale, *The Secret*, 2005) Sometimes it doesn't make sense to us how it will work. It doesn't add up on an intellectual level, but we trust what we feel. This process has paid off for us. My family uses the art of Feng Shui to visualize our goals and dreams, and we have been amazed with the results. I have clearly seen that when our home is out of balance, the corresponding area of our life is out of balance. If we want to create something but our home contradicts this, it can't show up. For instance, if we want to accumulate wealth and there is a fireplace in our wealth area, wealth will not show up. However adding a healthy tree and a water feature to the wealth area encourages the accumulation of wealth and it's interesting to watch it grow, just as the tree grows. Yes it is 90% intention, but this just shows us the power that we have to create with our intention.

Anybody can live in their ideal place. It doesn't matter who they are, what their background is, how much money they make; it is just about the images they hold in their mind. (*The Secret*) When we set our sights on anything, we can achieve it with no limits. So to me, the ideal place to live is the place that encourages this.

Have you ever known someone that moved into their dream home, but once they were there, it didn't feel like their dream home anymore? They have a large home in a nice neighborhood, but it doesn't look any different than their old place, they don't feel any different; the way maybe they thought they would feel? This is because they carry the same energy patterns with them; and until this energy pattern has changed, nothing will change.

This is a process that can't and won't happen until you are ready for it to. You must ask for it. When you are ready for change, Feng Shui is a great way to change the energy pattern. It doesn't matter if you have just moved or been in the same place for years, it is transforming. Once you decide that you are ready for change, it's time to define what you want in every area of your life. Create your life on purpose. This is your life!

The nine areas of the Ba Gua:

1. Health
2. Journey (aka Career)
3. Self-Knowledge / Wisdom
4. Family / Ancestry
5. Wealth / Abundance
6. Fame / Reputation
7. Relationships / Love
8. Children / Creativity
9. Helpful People Travel

I have numbered them in this way because this is the order we will walk through them. I will go into what each area means in the Ba Gua chapter, but I want you to be able to see the areas and start to become acquainted with them. The idea behind Feng Shui is that every area of your life is linked to these areas of your home. If you want to create wealth, a romantic relationship, become more creative, find a new job; there are certain areas of the Ba Gua that you will want to look at.

So here is the fun part. Now we get to walk through each area and actually create what we want. You will be able to specify exactly what it is that you want in the corresponding sector. Don't know exactly what you want? This is okay. You can remain open. You don't have to know the how; just identify the want. Want a better relationship with your spouse? Want to attract "the one"? Want more money? Want a new career or just to find your path? Here is a chance to create it. What is it that you want?

Define what you want in each area to look and feel like? Visualize it and watch it manifest. If we understand that it doesn't matter who we are, where we come from or what we might believe to be true about ourselves; then we can shift our thinking and visualize what we want, and it will show up. I have been amazed at the opportunities that have presented themselves to us through this process. I am a Certified Feng Shui Practitioner. I work with people every day. I practice this at home, and I very much believe in this practice. Once you open yourself up to "what if," your life will change.

What is your perfect place to live? If you had to define it, what would it look like? Would it be the place itself or the feeling of it? Could your perfect place be your little one room apartment with the old carpet? Could you find a different way to be grateful for what you have now, so that more things to be grateful for will show up? When we put ourselves in this place of gratitude, we get to experience more things to be grateful for. Look around at where you are right now, and list five things you love about where you are right now. Get creative if you have to, but let's start being grateful right now:

1._____
2._____
3._____
4._____
5._____

You will want a journal to begin this process every day. My favorite time to write in my gratitude journal is in the morning, so I can watch my day unfold feeling grateful. Another thing that is really important is to write down what you expect to manifest, in the now. These are the wishes that you have. Don't give thanks that they will show up tomorrow, this is about the now. This is a different "thank you" than the previous list. The previous list is what is surrounding you now; the following list is what you are manifesting:

I am so grateful for

_____

I am so grateful for

_____

I am so grateful for

_____

I am so grateful for

_____

I am so grateful for

_____

So to answer the question, what is Feng Shui, I would have to say it is recognizing that your environment and your life are connected, and that you can use your environment to help you create the life you want. To facilitate this, you must put your goals in front of your face and in your subconscious every day so that you will manifest your dreams and desires. Congratulations on taking this first step to creating the life you want!

Chapter 2
What Is Your Element?

I love creation--taking nothing and making it something, not stopping there, but making that something beautiful, extraordinary; then deciding what I want it to look like and watching it happen. This is one of the most powerful aspects of my Feng Shui adjustments. The first thing that I do when I work with clients is to element-type them. Once you understand your element and why you do what you do, you will understand yourself on a different level.

The first thing you want to do is identify your goals. What do you want to do with your life? Who do you want to be? We have no limits here; it is all about what you want. Answer this question on a soul level-- not considering if it is practical, but if it would fulfill your needs on a deeper level.

Joseph Campbell said, "Follow your bliss and the universe will open doors for you where there were only walls."

With this in mind, answer the question phrased this way:

If I could do anything with my life, I would
_____.

The answer you came up with should feel very good to you. Don't worry about how this will show up, just hold onto that good feeling that you have now. Doors will begin to open for you. You don't have to know how, but you will attract them. This is a fun exciting time.

The next thing that you want to do is take the *Five Element Assessment.*

FSTC's (The Feng Shui Training Center)
Five Element Assessment

Place the following scores in the blanks provided:

It is just like me = +3
It is somewhat like me = +1
It is unlike me = -2

____Be cautious and sensible (A)
____Enjoy frequent periods of solitude and introspection (A)
____Be content being anonymous or on the periphery of social events (A)
____Be considered self-absorbed (A)
____Be involved in intellectual pursuits (A)
____Be content figuring things out for myself (A)

____Be careful about what I reveal to other people (A)

____Be a stubborn defender of the truth as I see it (A)

____Be patient and persevering in spite of defeats and dead ends (A)

____Be objective and dispassionate (A)

____Feel self-sufficient in or out of a relationship (A)

____Choose privacy over intimacy, solitude over socializing (A)

____Remove myself from everyday affairs and turn inward to quietness (A)

____Reflect upon the place of my life in the grand scheme of things. (A)

Total A's _____

____Feel confident taking action (B)

____Feel powerful and invulnerable (B)

____Start new projects before I finish the previous one (B)

____Be comfortable with deadlines (B)

____Enjoy doing things that have never before been

____ done (B)

____ Act with confidence and assurance regardless of what others may think or feel (B)

____ Make quick decisions and change my mind often (B)

____ Be comfortable with tasks that demand "thinking on my feet" (B)

____ Be direct or provocative even if it causes discomfort or embarrassment to others (B)

____ Take pleasure in public recognition and admiration of my talents and achievements (B)

____ Be comfortable leading or directing others (B)

____ Follow my own hunches about what is right or wrong (B)

____ Take the lead when it is necessary to get things done quickly and effectively (B)

____ Feel comfortable guiding others and directing their efforts (B)

____ Disregard others' appraisals of me (B)

Total B's _____

____Be animated and enthusiastic (C)

____Enjoy the pleasure of my senses (C)

____Easily know what another thinks and feels (C)

____Be comfortable in a very stimulating environment (C)

____Openly share my inner most feelings and desires (C)

____Live in the here and now and not worry about the future or the past (C)

____See the humorous side of life (C)

____Be tender, intimate, and vulnerable with another person (C)

____Be comfortable receiving and showing affection and pleasure (C)

____Enjoy being moved emotionally (C)

____Interpret life's experiences through my emotional response to events (C)

____Easily become completely involved in the events going on around me (C)

____Become deeply identified with the feelings, thoughts, and experiences of another (C)

____Remain optimistic and hopeful in spite of what others may believe (C)

Total C's _____

____Be nurturing and supportive (D)
____Put the needs of others before my own (D)
____Take pains to preserve long-term relationships (D)
____Enjoy being relied upon for reassurance and help (D)
____Enjoy being the hub of my social and family network (D)
____Be agreeable and accommodating (D)
____Help people work together in a harmonious manner (D)
____Get involved in other people's lives (D)
____Enjoy maintaining many diverse, even conflicting relationships (D)
____Be diplomatic and tactful (D)
____Rely on the skill and intelligence of others (D)

____Accept other people's characterizations of who I am (D)

____Sympathize with the circumstances of other people (D)

____Get close enough to need another person (D)

Total D's ____

____Maintain a neat and orderly personal life-style (E)

____Be in control of my environment and the way I do things (E)

____Be strongly committed to my moral principles (E)

____Feel secure and confident in my work when I know that everyone is following proper procedures (E)

____Enjoy tasks that require systematic approaches to problem solving (E)

____Appreciate being thought of as meticulous and discriminating (E)

____Be self-contained and not overly involved in other people's affairs (E)

____Be appreciated or admired for my skill and expertise rather than my personality or emotional enthusiasm (E)

____Accept the authority of those with more competence (E)

____Be systematic and methodical in my work (E)

____Be content with few close attachments or demanding relationships (E)

____Put virtue and principles above pleasure and fulfillment (E)

____Restrain myself in expressing my feelings or opinions (E)

____Be tasteful and discriminating (E)

Total E's _____

A= Water Score _____

B= Wood Score _____

C= Fire Score _____

D= Earth Score_____

E= Metal Score_____

What your element is and what your goals are tells your story. This will let you know where you are in relation to your goal. If you want to start your own business, and your scores come back with no wood element, you will want to activate the wood element in yourself. If you are feeling depressed, you will find that your water is out of balance (the ability to go inside for answers). So, activating water in your home will help you to get to the root cause of why you are feeling depressed. Christine Delorey says that emptiness is our sad unfulfilled potential. The beautiful thing about the power these elements have is that we have the power to enhance what we need to meet our goals. We can look at our elements and plan around them. Or if we have something that we really want to do, but our element doesn't match it, we can enhance the element we need. It is that predictable.

Now I'm going to explain what being deficient, excessive and balanced looks like with the elements in our personality. As human beings, we seek to organize and order our world so that we can create meaning out of our experiences. We create categories and use those categories to make sense of our experiences. Chinese five-element theory provides a template for organizing our experiences according to five primary patterns: wood, fire, earth, metal and water. Knowing whether the power of wood, fire, earth, metal or water is preeminent sheds light on the goals we set, the risks we take, the competence we manifest, the postures we adopt towards people, the expectations we have, the things that most threaten us, and the satisfactions we receive. We will look at how these patterns manifest in a person's actions and body, and then discuss how to use these patterns to balance out excess and deficiencies by using the environment.

Water

Water is patient, enduring, quiet, and watchful. It finds a way around any obstacle and conserves energy to serve future needs. Water goes deep, desiring only to uncover the mysteries hidden within; oblivious to the mundane needs of daily life. Water holds itself in check; not acting on impulse or making decisions quickly. Water needs lots of time to think about the implications of decisions and the effect choices might have on society at large. Water is honest and lives by a strong honor code. It will not bend for the sake of momentary pleasures or ease. Preferring the long road to quick-and-easy fixes, water can sometimes prolong projects. Needing a container to take shape, water needs the focus of a project or purpose in order for chi to flow smoothly.

↑ Too much still water energy can result in depression and stagnation. You tend to be overly blunt, detached, and insensitive. This can also manifest as a tendency to be self-absorbed or lost in self-pity. Too much moving water can result in the feeling that life is passing you by; things are moving too quickly and you can't keep up. You resent the fact that you have no alone time and that others are interfering with your life in what seem to be trivial ways. It is difficult to show emotion and you suffer from isolation and feelings of loneliness. You tend to talk about the same ideas over and over but don't implement any of them.

⬇ Not enough water leaves you feeling cut off from the abundance and flow of life. This manifests as irritability, a tendency to be stingy, and a critical nature. You also have a difficult time feeling in tune with your emotions, and people find you superficial and "dry." Deficient water also leads to a loss of libido. You resist attachment and fear exposure.

☯ Just the right amount of water energy makes you watchful, clever, curious, careful, candid, and highly insightful. Whatever you have to say is well thought out and carries deep meaning. You are the quintessential philosopher. Your stillness and depth allow you to flush out ideas fully rather than bolting into new projects without careful planning. You are comfortable with the sacred and often help others see the spiritual implication of what they consider to be mundane or inconsequential choices. You are able to conceive of both new life and new ideas and carry those ideas and life forms into the world.

Wood

Wood energy surges upward, breaking through the earth's crust and pushing up into the sky. To overcome obstacles is its very reason for being. It represents the pioneer archetype, always looking for something new that's never been done before. New growth, new life, new projects excite wood energy. Wood energy is audacious and confident. It takes risks and responds well to pressure. As the liver stores and releases the blood, wood energy represents the release of chi into a project or purpose that then carries the chi to an outcome.

↑ An excess of wood results in burn out, the natural result of a tendency to overdo, over-perform and over-direct. Wood's desire to get things going and make things happen can result in frustration and impatience with those around you. Boldness can become aggressive and hostile, and the inability to rest and relax results in turbulent emotions and often anger. Wood's ability to be decisive and get things done can become impulsive and irresponsible if there is no metal (structure, rules) to temper its force. The excessive wood personality fears boredom and sameness above all.

↓ Without the driving motivating force of wood, it's easy to get lethargic, sluggish, and bogged down. Apathy is a direct response to a lack of wood energy. Sensitivity to noise, exhaustion, indecisiveness and general irritability are physical symptoms of inadequate wood energy. In periods of both excess and deficiency, wood is unable to maintain stable emotions. People with a lack of wood often look to others to know how they should feel in a given situation.

☯ Wood is bold, decisive and purposeful. A person with wood energy moves forward with confidence and attracts others as she journeys. The wood makes her strong and able to work through obstacles that would overwhelm someone else. She is a natural leader who encourages others to let go of their fear and move into self-actualization. Wielding power and influence comes naturally and she's not afraid of making decisions. She is forward thinking and has the ability to break ties and associations that no longer serve.

Fire

Fire energy is excitement, fullness, expression, warmth, and the ability to open up, expand, and radiate fullness. Fire also symbolizes wakefulness and the development of compassion. Through its connection with other life forms and energies, fire, more than any other pattern, expresses compassion for others and union with spirit. Transformation through fusion is the focus, and fire has the ability to merge disparate forces into one common element. Fire brings light, insight, love, and awareness into the world and can transform the mundane into the divine. Fire helps us understand how energy transforms from one form to another. As the flames transform substance into heat, it's easy to imagine how energy is transformed within the body and how we interact with the energy patterns in our homes.

↑ Too much fire and one loses a sense of self. The tendency to open and connect consumes and becomes of primary importance. This is the pleasure seeker who can't get enough stimulation and varied experiences. More sex, more closeness, more variety on the menu, new clothes, and continually looking to learn new things is an expression of excessive fire energy. This person is always learning but not spending the time to incorporate what he's learned in a meaningful way in the world. He flits along the surface of life's experiences, not wanting to invest the time or energy to dig deep into things. He fears separation and isolation.

⬇ Not enough fire and people are pale, cold, clammy, and unable to sustain body temperature. It's hard to get excited about anything and the natural result is to withdraw and isolate oneself. Without fire to open and expand the intellect, intuition becomes shaded and self doubts are common. This is commonly expressed as "being shy." A lack of fire also results in an inability to empathize with others; one feels a sense of dullness and heaviness and is unable to feel joy.

☯ Just the right amount of fire energy will keep you feeling motivated, alive, full of vitality, and connected to others. Fire helps people laugh easily, and feel the kind of joy that courses through the body. The right amount of fire opens the awareness and increases compassion for others. It leads to optimism and a general feeling of well-being and connectedness to all life.

Earth

We all need to be held and comforted, assured that we'll be taken care of and safe. Earth energy is the force that surrounds, stabilizes and reassures us that we are safe and everything is as it should be. This is the yin aspect of earth. Earth energy also provides a sense of solidity, the foundation upon which everything else is built. This yang aspect of earth is represented in rocks and mountains. Earth is the peacemaker, the stabilizing force that expends energy making sure that everyone's needs are met and that everyone feels safe and protected. Serenity and stability are ideal, and change is viewed as dangerous. Unification is the goal, not diversity.

⬆ Too much earth energy can be smothering and stifling (over-mothering). It creates rigidity and the inability to allow abundance (through change) into one's life. Because of its association with the spleen, excessive earth energy muddies thinking, leading to incessant worry, over-thinking and constant pondering. This can manifest as not wanting to do anything for fear of getting it wrong. Excessive earth is always worried about pleasing and pacifying others.

⬇ Not enough earth energy creates too much concern with survival needs to be open to explorations of an emotional and spiritual nature. Deficient earth energy manifests in a lack of grounding and stability in life. You have difficulty maintaining relationships for an extended period of time or tend to cling and act in an ingratiating manner. The "someone needs a hug" personality is lacking earth.

☯ A balanced flow of earth allows you to be nurturing but not overprotective; supportive and compassionate but not co-dependent. You feel grounded, secure, safe and comfortable with just about anybody. People feel instantly at home around you and tend to tell you their life story whether you ask or not. You can tolerate change but also like to take your time, making sure things are not rushed and that experiences are savored.

Metal

Without categories, we would not know how to create meaning in our lives. Metal understands this and works to create structure and order in otherwise random and chaotic experiences. The ability to distill or find the "essence" of something and structure randomness is the essence of metal.

↑ Too much metal energy can make the energy abrasive. Your desire to keep everything in its place gets in the way of normal living. For example, you can't go out in public with messy hair. You're always picking things apart and analyzing them to death. Nothing meets up to your expectations and people find you indifferent or aloof. At its extreme, metal cannot separate from ritualistic behaviors, which can lead to obsessive-compulsive disorders. You have a difficult time expressing emotion without sarcasm and feel impatient with others imperfections.

⬇ Not enough metal can make one feel unguarded and unprotected. Because metal increases one's ability to focus, not enough makes it difficult to focus or to follow an argument from start to finish. Physical appearance or work ethics tend towards sloppiness, and there seems to be no order or routine that applies. With deficient metal, you might find yourself bouncing from job-to-job or task-to-task without a strong sense of purpose.

☯ Just the right amount of metal energy allows for clear, well thought-out communication. You are methodical, disciplined, organized, honorable, discerning, and calm. You tend to understand the essence of others' communication and convey it back to them, providing greater insight and understanding. You are a natural scientist, relying on strict adherence to a method to verify and validate your findings.

Scoring

On the form on below, you will place your highest score in the kin spot (the element you are most like). You will then use the constructive cycle around the circle clockwise to fill in the blanks (i.e., fire always follows wood; metal always follows earth. See below.). Then add the scores in each of the sectors to create a fraction (see "Example of a Weak Chart" on the next page).

Constructive Cycle:

Water produces wood
Wood feeds fire
Fire makes earth
Earth creates metal
Metal holds water

Destructive Cycle:

Earth overcomes water
Water extinguishes fire
Fire melts metal
Metal cuts wood
Wood overcomes earth

Example of a Weak Chart:

I am supported by water (the Grantor).
I give my energy to fire (the Offspring).
I tend to dominate earth (the Subordinate).
I am restrained by metal (the Ruler).
I am similar in nature to wood (Kin).

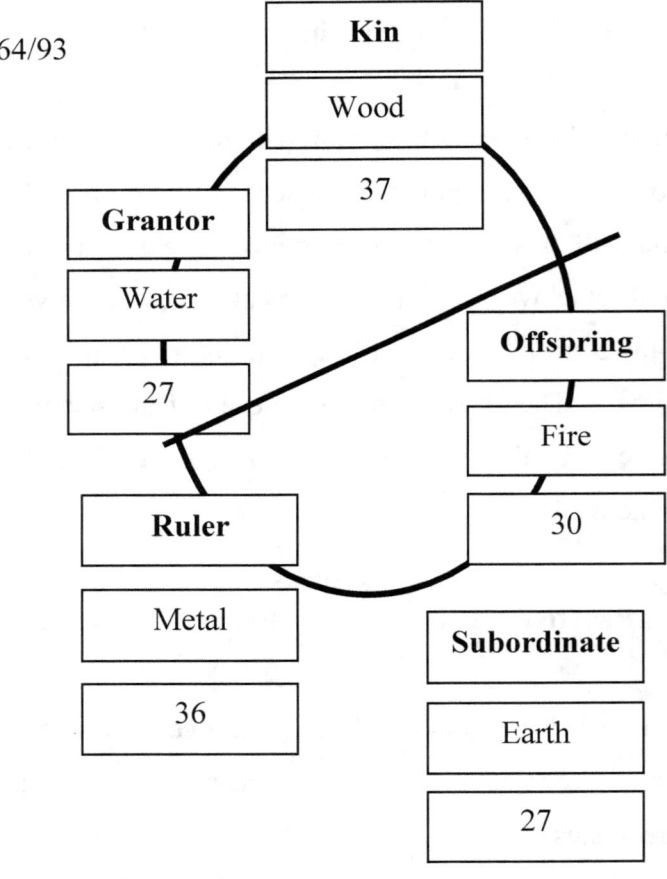

64/93

Explanation: 27 + 37 = 64   and   30 + 36 + 27 = 93, so the fraction is 64/93.

Now you try it!

I am supported by
_____.
(This element is the Grantor)

I give my energy to
_____.
(This element is the Offspring)

I tend to dominate
_____.
(This element is the Subordinate)

I am restrained by
_____.
(This element is the Ruler)

I am similar in nature to
_____.
(This element is Kin)

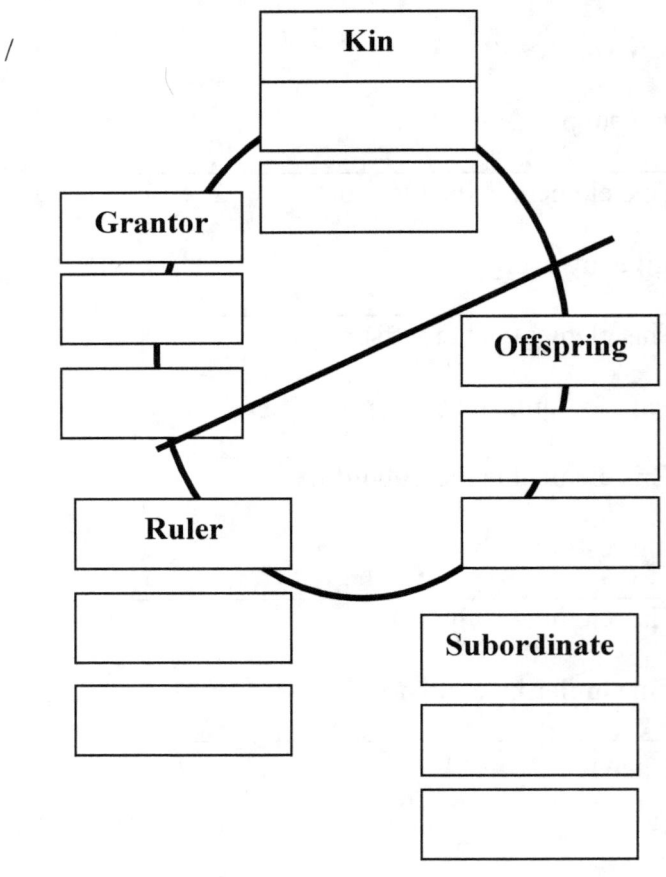

Ideally, you want the sector numbers balanced. If you have a much higher number on the top, you will find that you are in excess. If you have a higher number on the bottom, you will find you are deficient.

Pay attention to these elements. Not only are they in your body, they are in your environment. When we move into the Ba Gua, you will see that each area has an element. I want you to pay close attention to the constructive cycle and destructive cycle. This is critical when making adjustments! It's not hard to understand, but make sure your foundation in this is strong to avoid mistakes!

The Water Element is found in:

- Streams, rivers, pools, fountains and water features of all kinds.
- Reflective surfaces, such as cut crystal, glass and mirrors.
- Flowing, free form and asymmetrical shapes.
- The black and dark-tone spectrum of colors, such as charcoal gray and midnight blue.

Water energy represents wealth in Feng Shui – it brings prosperity.

The Wood Element is found in:

- Wooden furniture and accessories
- Wooden paneling, siding, roofing and decks.
- All indoor and outdoor plants and flowers, including silk and plastic.
- All types of plant-based cloth and textiles, such as cotton and rayon.
- Floral print upholstery, wall coverings, drapes and linens.
- Art depicting landscapes, gardens, plants and flowers.
- Columnar shapes, such as columns, pedestals and poles.
- Paper
- Color is green.

Wood energy brings growth, expansion and management; luck of material success.

The Fire Element is found in:

- All lighting, including electric, oil, candles, natural sunlight and fireplaces.
- Shapes such as triangles, pyramids and cones.
- The red spectrum of colors – red tones, red-orange and maroon.

Fire energy brings expansion. It offers success in public life, fame and recognition.

The Earth Element is found in:

- All rocks and stones, adobe, brick, tile and crystals.
- Ceramic or earthenware objects.
- Shapes such as squares, rectangles and long flat surfaces.
- Pets and wildlife.
- Art that depicts people, animals and earthy landscapes of desert or fertile fields.
- The yellow and earth tone spectrum of colors.

Earth energy brings stability, firmness, reliability and dependability; grounding energy; it epitomizes the heart of Feng Shui.

The Metal Element is found in:

- All types of metal, including stainless steel, copper, brass, iron, silver, aluminum and gold.
- Art and sculpture made from metal.
- Shapes of the circle, oval and arch.
- The white and light pastel spectrum of colors.

Metal energy brings luck of powerful and helpful people in your life; power and great influence.

Finally, spend some time studying the elements so that you gain an understanding about what works together and what doesn't. You will want to understand how to use the constructive and destructive cycles to your benefit. Play with these elements; this will help you in the creation process. Have fun with this!

Chapter 3
The Ba Gua

For thousands of years, the Chinese have studied what happens to energy as it flows through a physical space. One of their most astounding discoveries is that there is a predictable pattern, a relationship, between different physical locations in your home and different aspects of your life. For example, there is a certain part of your home that relates directly to your personal abundance, another to your career, and another to your intimate relationships. If a part of your home is missing, no energy flows to that aspect of your life. On the other hand, if a part of your home receives a lot of energy and attention, that area of your life blossoms. This map of how energy flows through a physical space is called the Ba Gua. To bring harmony and balance into your life, you need to balance out the energy flow through the rooms of your home. Use the Ba Gua map to understand which areas of your home relate to which life sectors.

We will start with the health, which is in the center because this is our foundation, so to speak. If we don't have our health, or if we aren't stable and grounded; none of the rest really matters. The center not being balanced can show up as poor health or even trouble paying bills. This is your foundation, and it is extremely important to get this part right. I'm not giving you permission to be stressed about it; just be aware of it. As we go through each sector, I want you to notice what it represents and what the element is.

Abundance (Wealth)	External Recognition (Fame)	Intimate Relations (Commitment and Marriage or Partnership with Co-workers)
Wood	Fire	Earth
Purple (Rich Jewel Tones)	Red / Bright Colors	Pink (Soft Tones, but no Peach)
Ancestors (Family of Origin)	Health (Tai Chi)	Creative Offspring (Children)
Wood	Earth	Metal
Green	Yellow	White / Rainbow Colors
Self-knowledge (Wisdom)	Journey (Career)	Helpful People & Community (Travel)
Earth	Water	Metal
Blue / Brown	Black / Dark Blue	Gray / Silver

This is What the Ba Gua Map Actually Looks Like

You simply put the Ba Gua map over a floor plan of your home. Notice if you have any missing sectors or if you have some extra. I am going to put a number by each sector as I list them below. The *only* reason I am numbering them this way is that this is the order in which I like to work in homes. The reason is because I like to create stability first, and then move into the journey, where new opportunities, ideas and sometimes careers are born. We move around the Ba Gua in a way that supports you on your new journey; to me, this makes the most sense.

Health / Center (1): At the physical center of the home, the health sector is where the energies of all other sectors combine and balance. As such, it should be as open and free from encumbrances (walls, furniture, and hallways) as possible. It's no surprise that the health sector is governed by the earth element, representing our ability to nurture and support ourselves. Physical health is at the heart (center) of our abilities to manifest and be present in all other areas of our lives. It means being in your body, listening to its voice and bringing its needs into balance with the rest of your life. The health sector is related to balance--all things in balance. Find a piece of art that you are drawn to, and which represents what you want to create in your life. If it has circles in it, all the better. Make sure it is something that makes you feel good and balanced when looking at it. If it doesn't have any circles in it, you can cut out a circle and write on the circle how balanced, healthy and abundant your family is and place it on the back of the picture.

Journey (2): This is the start of each new journey, decision or life path. Often referred to as the career sector, this should actually be thought of, as a life path. This area has more to do with your journey and the alignment of the soul than it does a chosen career. However, enhancing this sector will certainly enhance your career. But beware! It can also "wake you up" to your particular life journey, resulting in a change in your career if it isn't in alignment with your particular life purpose. I'm not trying to scare you. This is exciting! Who doesn't want to be on their life path?

Making a life out of feeding your soul; how does it get any better than that? That is what this sector is about.

I always suggest practicing being wrong about things you think you know. This brings in more opportunity. If you know everything, what is there to learn? Pose the question "what if" and you fill in the blank afterward. (What if I am smart enough to go back to school? What if I could start a business?) Go back to childhood and find that faith that you lost. It is okay to dream. That is how we find our path! If you don't have dreams; what do you have? The answers you come up with will change the way you look at life. This area is represented by water; the color is black; and the shapes are flowing, free form and asymmetrical.

Wisdom / Self-Knowledge (3): The energy of self-knowledge is the process of distinguishing the self from the watery abyss of the journey Gua. Associated with the element of earth, this sector encourages the process of individuation. As the infant realizes he is separate from mother, individuation starts to occur. This process involves setting clear boundaries and distinguishing your needs from the needs of those around you. As the mountain, you must learn to be still, centered, grounded and feel your own strength. As your water comes up, you begin to go inside and the ideas come flooding in. This area will support you in your journey. Where do you want to gain knowledge from? Who do you want to gain knowledge from? No limiting beliefs here; no boundaries and no judgment. Put things here--even a simple piece of paper that will encourage you to identify where you want to gain knowledge from. Going inside will direct you. The color for this area is blue; the element is earth; and the shape is square.

Family (4): Having individuated yourself in the self-knowledge Gua, the family Gua helps you discover who you are within the context of the family. This Gua holds the accumulated power of all those who made it possible for you to be here and provides opportunities for your continued growth. This Gua represents how the family forms the foundation for individual growth. The element is wood; the color is green; and the shape is a vertical rectangle (wide).

Abundance (5): As the branches of a tree receive the movement of the wind, this sector represents your ability to open to and receive the bounties of the universe. If you've ever had a day when you were doing what you absolutely loved, and ended the day feeling more energized than you began, you've experienced this energy pattern. Abundance energy encourages us to be more fully ourselves, to live our dreams and give our gifts. This Gua is often associated with material wealth, and it's true that money can greatly facilitate the pursuit of dreams. However, focusing on money often prevents us from seeing the abundance that is present all around us. By acknowledging the numerous manifestations of abundance, our relationship with money often changes as well. The element wood governs this Gua; the color is purple or jewel tones; and the shape is vertical rectangle (thin).

Fame / Reputation (6): As we give our gifts fully and joyfully to the world, the world recognizes our accomplishments and efforts. This sector is your fame area, the place where you shine. It represents how you want to be recognized for what you spend your life's energy doing. It also gives the world a way to say thank you and to affirm that what you're doing with your life is valuable. This recognition is not always in the form of certificates or awards. It can be heart-felt thank you cards from friends or drawings from children; anything that expresses appreciation. The fame sector is governed by the fire element, the color red and the triangle shape. What do you want to be known for? This is an important question to ask. Remember this area is directly linked to your journey area and abundance. Get specific about it, and remember that it can always be changed.

Relationships (7): Ruled by the earth element, this area of your home is dedicated to your connection with mother earth and other members of the human race. It represents your ability to make a commitment to something outside yourself: a career, a home, the earth or another person. After reaching your personal zenith (fame), you move into the interpersonal side of the Ba Gua cycle. It is related to the earth and encourages you to develop relationships of trust, intimacy and openness. The element that governs this Gua is earth; the color is pink; and the shape is square.

Creativity / Goals / Future (8): The natural result of receiving the supportive and nurturing energy of the intimate relations Gua is a burst of creative energy. Sometimes this energy manifests in the birth of children; sometimes in other creative undertakings. This is the playground of childhood. You might have literal children who need a space where it's okay to play, explore, create and destroy those creations. Regardless, you need that type of space yourself. A place where you don't take yourself or the world too seriously; a place to mess around--try things out and start over if you don't like it. This sector is also related to the metal element, and as such is concerned with the creation of new things--especially intellectual ideas. This area can also be thought of as goals, vision and your future! The colors here are the pastel rainbow spectrum, and the shape is a circle or half moon.

Helpful People / Travel (9): At the end of the life cycle is the time for sharing your gifts, not only with a spouse and immediate children, but also with an entire community. Governed by the metal element, this sector helps you draw together the various pieces of your life's story and forge a chalice into which you pour all that you have learned and become along the way. This chalice is your ability to give and receive aid from others. This area of your home relates to your connection to a universal life force, your visible and invisible means of support and your sense of community. Related to the heavens, this cosmic energy encourages you to call for aid from spiritual communities and heavenly beings, as well as physical neighbors. Coming at the age of retirement, this Gua is strongly connected to travel.

Notice that each sector of the Ba Gua has a dominant element. You should be a master at the elements, so activating these sectors with the benefit of the elements should be a breeze. I also would like you to realize that you can be as creative as you would like. You don't like trees, but want the cash flow? In the abundance, try some wide stripes painted on the wall (yang wood). Your front door is in your journey sector and you have a beautiful wooden door. Can't paint it? Think of the door as your wood element being activated; making you strong; looking for new exciting things that haven't been done before. Bring in a water feature or even a black mat at your front door (black = water)!

Recognize the symbolism in this process and let your adjustments fit who you are. Don't fall into the trap that there is only one way to do this. There are endless ways to achieve balance, abundance and to fulfill all of your dreams. As long as you understand how the elements work and what is destructive, follow that pattern, and you will be fine. I find when working with clients that when an adjustment resonates with them, it is much more effective. Go to the forum (www.thefengshuitrainingcenter.com/studentlounge) and throw some ideas out there. Pay attention to other ideas, the results will amaze you. Have fun being creative. This is your life!

Okay, so pull out the floor plan of your home, or draw it to scale. We will start with the "mouth of chi," or the front door. The Ba Gua is positioned according to "the mouth of chi." For an entire home, the mouth of chi is the architectural front door (where the house numbers are displayed). The front door serves as the face of the house, the transition space between the chi of the environment and the chi of the house.

Position the Ba Gua map so that the front door is either aligned with the self knowledge, journey, or helpful people sectors. To do this, go outside and stand facing the house. If the front door is on the left side of the house, then you enter your space through the self knowledge sector. If the front door is in the middle of the house, you enter into journey. And if the front door is on the right side, you enter into Helpful People. These three Guas form the front line of the Ba Gua (sometimes referred to as the Kan line.) Assuming the house is rectangular, the rear right Gua will be intimate relations; the rear middle Gua is external recognition; and the rear left Gua is abundance.

Does the Garage Count?

One of the most popular questions! When determining whether or not to include your garage in your Ba Gua, consider how fully integrated into your living space your garage is. If there are living areas either above or below the garage, and if the garage shares the same roofline as the house, it functions as part of the living space and needs to be included in the Ba Gua. Garages are typically yin spaces (not much active living happens there) and can create problems similar to missing sectors.

What About More Than One Level?

The Ba Gua is applied according to how chi enters and flows through the space. Therefore, each level of your home has a separate Ba Gua depending on the direction of chi flow. For an upstairs level, stand on the top stair and hold the Ba Gua map out in front of you. If you are standing in the center of the house, whatever's directly in front of you is the external recognition sector; the area in front of you on the right is intimate relations; the area in front on the left is abundance. Whatever is behind you on your left is your self knowledge sector; the area behind you on the right is helpful people; and directly behind you in the center is journey. Health is always in the center. The same directions apply for a lower level, except that you stand on the bottom step to position the Ba Gua.

Missing Sector?

Irregular shapes don't always create missing sectors. In general, if the existing portion is at least half the width of the house, it has enough density to pull energy in on the other side of the house, creating a missing piece. If the existing portion is less than half, it projects energy outward, but doesn't create an inward pull. Therefore, the piece is a projection and there is nothing missing.

Okay, now on to the examples:

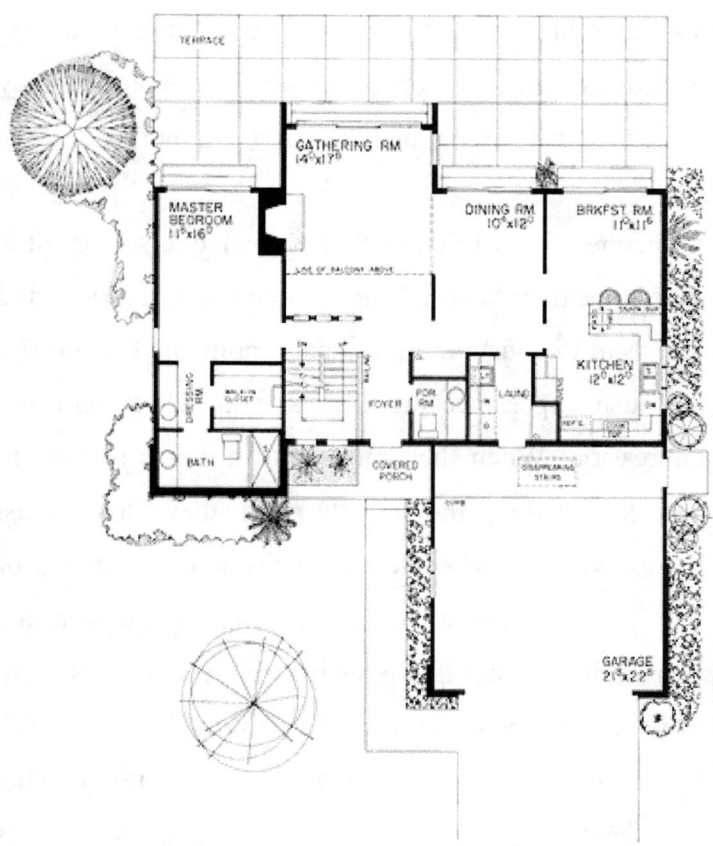

Here we have a home with missing journey and self knowledge sectors. Let me explain how this can show up. A missing journey (career) sector can mean troubles in getting or keeping a job. Since journey is also related to new beginnings, and a willingness to start over, a missing career sector can correspond with a mid-life crisis in males. Often they feel like they want to start over, but lack direction and purpose.

Someone with a missing Self Knowledge sector often finds that they have no alone time. Spouse, kids, and job seem to consume every spare moment. This person can also experience difficulties with self-esteem and depression. When they move into a house lacking in self knowledge, they might find they don't trust themselves to make their own decisions anymore or that they struggle with maintaining appropriate boundaries. What is interesting about this assessment of what happens is that I have seen it in clients. I don't know them, go to the home and tell them this is what their home is saying about them. Their story matches what I have just described to them. It is amazing how accurate it is.

The following home is full of issues (staircase in the center, facing the door, bathroom in the center, garage in the wealth), but we will address the missing part of the fame / reputation area and all of the relationship area later.

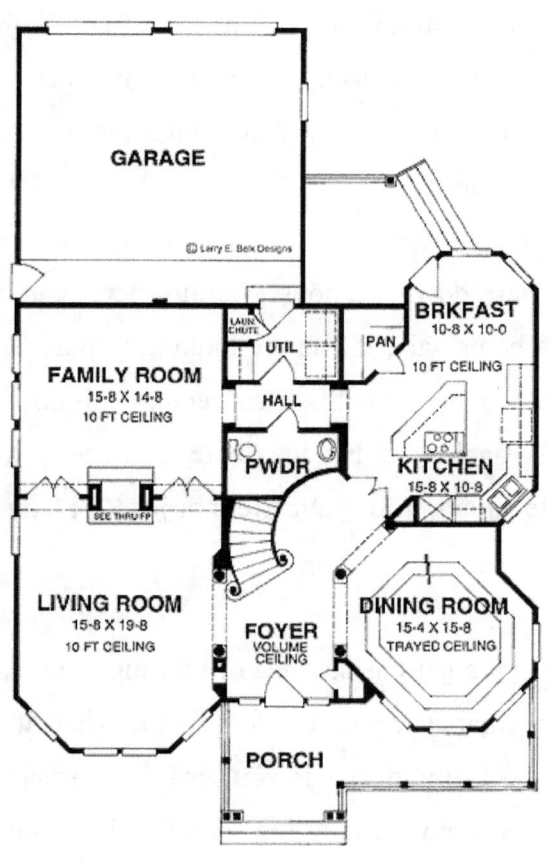

When the energy of support and commitment is missing, all kinds of things can go awry. Spouses cheat on each other. Women turn to food or shopping for support; men turn to work or sports. If the marriage is solid enough to withstand the turbulence, often it's the children that reflect the lack of support. They act out (often physically), quit half-way through something, or attract flaky friends.

No need to burn down the house. Adjustments can be made. That being said, if you are looking to purchase or move into a home with these sectors missing, I would advise against it. The idea here is to set up the best possible situation for your life; not just to plan on fixing it.

Now that you are getting the idea of missing sectors, I will explain what it means to each sector when it is missing. Keep in mind that if you have a destructive element in a certain area, it can manifest just like a missing sector. For example, a fire place in your wealth area manifests like a missing wealth area.

Journey (Career). When this Ba Gua sector is missing, it can mean troubles in getting or keeping a job. Since Journey is also related to new beginnings, and a willingness to start over, a missing career sector can correspond with a mid-life crisis in males. Often they feel like they want to start over, but lack direction and purpose.

Self Knowledge. Someone with a missing Self Knowledge sector often finds that they have no alone time. Spouse, kids, and job seem to consume every spare moment. This person can also experience difficulties with self-esteem and depression. When they move into a house lacking in self knowledge, they might find they don't trust themselves to make their own decisions anymore or that they struggle with maintaining appropriate boundaries.

Family and Ancestors. When this Ba Gua sector is missing, family issues tend to go unresolved. They burrow underground and fester. Siblings, parents, or children get their feelings hurt and don't call each other for months or sometimes years. People also miss the support and the sense of belonging that comes from family-of-origin relationships.

Abundance and Wealth. A lack of energy in personal abundance and wealth results in the feeling that there is not enough. Not enough time. Not enough money. Not enough energy. It's as if the person has been cut off from the source and life dries up, feels blasé. Activities tend to tire more than excite or rejuvenate. Money is spent fixing problems (leaky faucet, medical bills, credit cards) more than enjoying life. It feels too risky to do something one really enjoys because of an ever-present fear that life will snatch enjoyment away, like a parent snatching candy away from a child.

External Recognition. A missing External Recognition sector manifests in the feeling that nothing the person does is appreciated or truly valued. Things are taken for granted, or others take credit for something they didn't do. For married couples, both people tend to feel that they are doing more than their share, and children feel like they can't please parents, no matter what.

Creative Offspring. An absence in this area can manifest in stymied creativity or the inability to conceive children. In general, one feels unable to give their gifts to the world for one reason or another. It can take the form of a boss who refuses to give the person riskier, more creative projects. It can take the form of no time to paint, shoot photos, or write that book. And it can take the form of an empty cradle.

Helpful People. If this sector is missing, one finds the connection to things greater than himself lacking.

There is no sense of community or belonging outside of the family unit. Earlier in life, this lack can appear as a dearth of opportunities and friends--no mentors, no supporters, no trustworthy business partners. Later in life, this lack looks more like isolation. The communities the person participated in when younger have dissolved, and no new ones have taken their place. For young and old, there is a sense that life is stuck; there's no going anywhere.

Enhancing Ba Gua Sectors

If you find that you do have a section missing in your home, or that a sector doesn't receive as much energy as you would like it to, you can restore balance by directing energy to that area. For the adjustments to be as effective as possible, follow the processes outlined for each adjustment below but feel free to substitute adjustment items that resonate with your life style, your experiences, and your cultural and personal symbolism.

General Adjustments

Depending on your situation, you might need to adjust for a missing sector either outside or inside the house. If you're living in an apartment, for example, the missing sector might be your neighbor's living room. In that case, you'll need to work from within your own living space.

Exterior Adjustments

- Locate the place outside the house where the walls would come if the section wasn't missing. Place a spotlight in that exact location and shine it up at the roofline of the house.
- Build an actual structure in the missing area, such as a deck, brick patio, or garden arbor.
- Plant trees or bushes in the missing area.
- Bring sound energy into the area with wind chimes.
- Bring hydraulic energy to the area by adding an outdoor fountain.

- Stabilize the chi flow by adding large boulders or raised beds in the missing area.
- A rock garden in the missing sector is a great idea for homes that have a long winter season. The rocks will stabilize the chi whether there's sun or snow.
- Place a bench or chair in the area to draw people out there more often.
- Add a stone or metal birdbath. The birds will bring living chi to the area and the metal and stone will stabilize it. Be sure not to let the water stagnate.

You can also adjust missing sectors from inside the house:

Interior Adjustments

- Place a mirror on an existing wall that directs energy towards the missing section.
- The Ba Gua can be placed on an individual room as well as the entire house. To balance

out a missing sector in the house, place an energizing object (lamp, mirror, plant, etc.) in the corresponding sector of a room that relates to the missing sector. For example, if your abundance sector is missing, place a lamp in the abundance corner (rear left) of your office. If your intimate relations sector is missing, place a healthy growing plant in the intimate relations corner (rear right) of your bedroom.
- For a partially missing sector, bring a sound system or other sound generator (wind chimes, gongs, bells) into the existing portion.

Remember that you want your adjustments to feel good to you. Get as creative as you would like. They will be more powerful this way. Keep in mind each element's constructive and destructive cycles so that you do things in a beneficial way.

Chapter 4
What Are You Going To Create?
(Your Three Objectives)

What are you going to create? Before starting your Feng Shui journey, sit down and decide three things you want to create. If you are working with a practitioner, make sure he/she uses this method. You wouldn't plan a vacation without a destination would you? Be specific, but not so attached to the way it has to look that you couldn't miss it. When we are open to possibilities, the possibilities become endless. The universe is always sending us opportunities. Sometimes they come in a form we may perceive as tragedy or annoyance, or we just overlook it because it doesn't appear like we had envisioned. When we approach these situations with our mind open, we are on our path; and will be amazed at the opportunities that present themselves and the people that rush in to help us. I will share our objectives with you; challenge you to come up with your own; and tailor your plan to fit your objectives.

Our Objectives

- Use Our Gifts
- Follow Our Purpose On Our Journey
- Build Our Business

Objective #1 – Use Our Gifts. Yes, this one is vague; we all have gifts, countless gifts. Which ones do we want to use? All of them! We all have special talents and abilities and they are unique to us. When we focus on someone else's gifts we might try to use them, but in the process waste our own. The objective here is to be so in tune with ourselves that we feel our gifts, and have the ability to use them in faith. You should also recognize that gifts grow when they are used. Sometimes we might try something for a while, and then decide it doesn't fit anymore. This is okay; it might just be a stepping-stone to get to our next step. Go easy on yourself, we are always learning and growing.

We will address this objective in the:

- Center of the home to have a strong foundation, being centered and balanced
- Wisdom/self knowledge to open us up to learning, and listening to our spirit
- Helpful people area, inviting others to help us on this journey, pointing the way

Objective #2 - Follow Our Purpose On Our Journey. Paul and I recognized our gifts to work together to compliment each other's strengths and strengthen each other's weaknesses in our Feng Shui business and in our life. We both have a passion for this work because of the peace and comfort we find in it. We knew a great way to stimulate the growth in our purpose was to renew our home. Our home was beautiful; everything about it was great--the paint, the window coverings, the furniture, and the art. However five years into it, we needed something new. After all, it had served its purpose. It had brought us to this crossroads. We discovered that as beautiful as our home was, it wasn't us; or at least the "us" that was occupying it now. We wanted a fun playful environment not only for us, but also for our children. We wanted everyone to play, create and re-create in it. We decided to follow the Ba Gua to a tee. Wood sections were painted a wood color; fire was painted fire colors; however this time, we used a fire blue instead of red. Earth was earth or fire, metal was metal. We wanted to see what else we would create in our life. We wanted to follow our purpose, and of course be open to what that might look and feel like. We have short and long-term goals, but they are not set in stone. Being open allows more room for opportunity to find its way to our front door!

We will address this objective in the:

- Center – being on purpose requires us to be centered and grounded
- Journey – open to what this journey will look like
- Wisdom / Self Knowledge – connecting with our spiritual side and letting it guide us

- Relationship – a strong relationship between the two of us and our children is essential to following our purpose
- Creativity – creating and re-creating ourselves until we find what fits

Objective # 3 – Build Our Business. When it finally came out of my mouth that I wanted to become a Feng Shui Practitioner, I knew a few things:

- I knew it worked.
- I knew I had a knack for it.
- I knew I wanted to do this for the rest of my life.
- I knew that I needed to become certified.

But there were things I didn't know:

- How would I pay for school?
- Where would I get clients?
- How would I advertise?

You know the big things! I kept hearing it was about having faith that it would all work out. I knew that when you ask for something and keep doing the next thing, that everything falls into place, but knowing that and actually doing it are two different things. I teach people all the time to follow their dreams, go with their gut, listen to themselves and they will never go wrong. Could I follow my own advice? I had to! How could I ask something from someone else that I couldn't do myself?

We will address this objective in the:

- Journey – open to what this journey will look like.
- Reputation – I knew that I needed to be known as "The Feng Shui Lady"!
- Helpful People – I needed assistance from many helpful people to accomplish this. I couldn't build a business by myself.
- Relationships – I needed sound relationships with all those with whom I work.

When you start making adjustments in your home, you don't just paint or place an object in the correct corner and then poof, your life changes. It is a process. If you are having trouble with money and you activate your wealth corner, you might find unexpected cash. However, if your relationship with money isn't changed, you will find yourself in the same situation again. The key is to be open to learning why your relationship with money is the way it is. Let this rise to the surface and deal with it so that you can move into extravagance. The fun part isn't the end result—it's the process of getting there! Things come up that you have to deal with; things you don't realize need to be dealt with. You must come into alignment with what you are striving to be. You will notice how things that aren't in alignment will fall away. Get ready! It's a fun process, but it is work.

So now it is your turn. What three things do you want to create?

1. _____
2. _____
3. _____

Objective#1_____

will be addressed in the following sectors of the Ba Gua.

- _____
- _____
- _____
- _____
- _____

Objective#2_____

        will be addressed in the following sectors of the Ba Gua.

- _____
- _____
- _____
- _____
- _____

Objective#3_____

        will be addressed in the following sectors of the Ba Gua.

- _____
- _____
- _____
- _____
- _____

Remember, these patterns are predictable. You have the power right now to design your life. There are no mistakes here, put it in pencil, you can always change it as your goals change.

I have some clients that give me three different phrases of the same need for all three objectives. Expand yourself, don't think that by finding "the one" your life will all come together or that money will make you happy. This is about balance; it is as simple as that.

Once your goals are defined and you start to put adjustments in place, make sure you spend some time there acknowledging what it is you are creating and giving thanks for the things you are creating that you don't yet realize.

Three Secrets Reinforcement

The Three Secrets Reinforcement used by most Feng Shui practitioners is a blessing and empowering ritual that is done with each of your Feng Shui adjustments and cures. Although the cures will work without the blessing, they will work quicker and more effectively with it. This three step blessing opens a flood of chi / energy, directing it into the adjustment you've made, giving you very powerful results.

Body: The first part of the blessing consists of the *Mudra*. This refers to a hand position, which directs the chi into your cure.

Heart: To calm the mind, bring peace and create harmony. Place left hand on top of your right hand, palms up, thumbs touching, in front of your heart area.

Praying hands: To add auspicious energy and good fortune. Hands together in front of your heart area.

Speech: The second part of the blessing is the *Mantra*. This simply put, refers to words of power, or a kind of prayer. The one you choose is repeated softly, out loud, 9 times.

Heart Sutra:
> Gate (Gah Tay) – gone
> Gate (Gah Tay) – gone
> Paragate (Pahra Gah Tay) – Completely Gone
> Parasamgate (Pahra Sahm Gah Tay) – Completely Across Gone
> Bodhi – Bringing in the blessings
> Svaha – And so it is

Others: From your own religious or spiritual tradition.

Mind: The third and final step is the **Visualization**. The visualization process allows you to focus the intent, purpose, or result that you want into the adjustment that you've made.

The three secrets reinforcement directs a powerful stream of chi/energy into your Feng Shui cures. It is important that you remember to do this blessing, as you want to be sure to get the best results possible from your Feng Shui adjustments.

Five years into my Feng Shui journey, I hired a Practitioner to come in and take a look at what I had done and see what I was missing. With my knowledge, I knew enough to play with it, but not enough to see my own stuff. She came in and gave me a list of things to get changed, blessed the home and left. I promptly completed the list, and waited. These were simple things that I couldn't see, because I lived there every day. Within 2 weeks, Paul decided to go back to school, for Business Management, and within 6 months I had decided to become a Feng Shui Practitioner and start my own business. In less than a year from having the Practitioner come out, Paul had joined me in this business venture. Within 2 ½ years we had bought the Feng Shui Training Center, our long term goal. Things were moving quickly. I could have never anticipated the changes in our life, nor would I have wanted to. It was like Christmas every day. Not that we never hit bumps in the road, but we were on this incredible journey together and we could not anticipate from one moment to the next what incredible thing would happen. We had just decided to be open to *what if* and being open paid off!

As mentioned earlier, Christine DeLorey says that emptiness is our own sad unfulfilled potential. We don't fulfill our potential because we are closed. When we are open to what if, the possibilities really are unlimited. There are some things that you will know that you want to create, be specific about these things. The things you aren't completely set on leave some opportunity for the universe to give you more than you would have thought to ask for.

Congratulations on completing the first step in your Feng Shui journey. You have made important steps by putting your goals in writing. As you walk through each area of Ba Gua and make your adjustments, you will see how you truly are creating your life from the outside in. Enjoy this process and have fun!

Chapter 5
The Center

The most common request I see in my practice is the desire for money. Even those that don't understand Feng Shui want to know how to manifest that winning lottery ticket. This is sad in a way; we place money above so much. We have bought the lie that if we are rich enough, thin enough, pretty enough, etc; then we will be happy, and money is of course on the top of the list. Once we "get" the concept that our happiness comes from within, and being on our path and not someone else's; this will free us from unnecessary limitations. Once the comparison goes away and we judge ourselves by our standards and not those of others, everything will change. The source that we will be coming from will open the doors necessary to make our hopes and dreams our reality. That source is in each of us, it is us. Once you are in this place and understand that you find happiness within yourself, it is actually easier to draw money to you. Like attracts like, so when you are in a place of gratitude, happiness and balance; you are going to attract more things that affirm these feelings.

I teach a class on creating abundance with Feng Shui. Abundance isn't just about money; it's about time, love, friends, and of course, balance. If you had more money than you could ever spend and no one to share it with, would you enjoy it? If you didn't support charities close to your heart and held onto it as if this was all you would ever get, would it feed your soul? If your soul isn't fed you won't be happy. You will feel as if something is missing. Balance is key to creating abundance, and tapping into your "source" is the fastest way to get there.

When I put on my "Feng Shui" eyes in a client's home, it is always an amazing story. Everyone has a story and it's always remarkable when adjustments are made and you can watch the shifts take place before your eyes. It is predictable. Most clients that are having trouble making ends meet think they need to work in the abundance area of the home. I want you to understand that the abundance area is really about more than meeting ends; it is about extravagance. The day-to-day flow of the home will come from the center, which is your foundation; the place from which things are built. All areas of the Ba Gua must be balanced or abundance won't flow. I want you to understand that when I say abundance, I am speaking on all levels--not just monetary. You can have more money than you can ever spend, but if you don't have abundance in other areas: relationships, health, creativity; how much fun is that money really going to be? If you aren't doing what you are passionate about, and you don't enjoy waking up every day; what kind of a life is that?

When you activate a sector of your home, this is going to start a chain reaction. You are asking for something and if you are blocking the flow of it, things will surface for you to move through so that you can receive it. If you aren't in alignment with what you are asking for, you won't receive it. What is neat about this process is that we begin to see changes within ourselves. Sometimes they feel uncomfortable, but it is a growing process. This is the time to go inside and see what is shifting and embrace it.

At the physical center of the home, the health sector is where the energies of all the other sectors combine and balance. As such, it should be as open and free from encumbrances (walls, furniture, hallways) as possible. It's no surprise that the health sector is governed by the earth element, representing our ability to nurture and support ourselves. Physical health is at the heart (center) of our ability to manifest and be present in all other areas of our lives. It means being in your body, listening to its voice, and bringing its needs into balance with the rest of your life. The health sector represents balance, all things in balance.

I want you to locate the center of the Ba Gua in your home. What is there? If it is clutter, clear it out. Locate the health area of the Ba Gua; find the center of that center. Find something circular for this spot. A rug, a table, a picture or anything that feels right to you. Let this be the center and affirm those feelings you want to feel every day. Watch how things start to shift and how different you begin to feel. This is intention in action. What do you want to feel like? Do you want more energy? Does life feel stressful and overwhelming? How different would you feel if you didn't focus on what you don't want? What if you shifted your focus to what you do want? This is the ideal place to start this process. As you begin to be grateful for what is working in your life, you will notice that more things show up to be grateful for. This is going to set the tone for the rest of your adjustments. So have fun with this, be creative and open. This would be a great thing to write about in your gratitude journal, especially if you are lacking in your earth element. Remember that your earth element is your ability to take care of yourself.

The color for this sector is yellow, but I want you to think outside the box a bit here. It would get a bit boring if everyone had the same color choices for each sector of the Ba Gua. What we are trying to achieve here are elements. Although there are specific colors associated with each area of the Ba Gua, they don't have to be visible. Why don't we try a square (square

= earth) picture that has some yellow in it? What if you don't like yellow? Put a piece of yellow paper behind that square picture. Go back to the elements chapter and look at what represents earth and get creative. This is the fun part; the creation process.

Since the center of the home is your starting point, the shifts will now begin to happen. Take time here to assess this Gua of the home. I can't stress enough the importance of having this area clean, clear and open. Being open here will help you become balanced and once the center is balanced, it is so much easier to create balance throughout the rest of your home and life.

Here are some questions to look at before working in the center of the home:

- How is your health (emotional, physical, and spiritual)?
- How is your energy level?
- How are your finances?

Focusing on what you want in these areas is important. Focus on the end result, not the lack. (Remember, we get what we focus on). Another choice in your "center piece" in this space is a piece of art with earthy tones, circles or something that just says balance to you. You want to feel it when you see it. This will make the adjustment much more powerful. Avoid trees here or vertical rectangles, since wood breaks up the earth.

Once you have completed this area of the home, you will move into the journey area. But please, get this area balanced first. This is your foundation, take your time and get this done right from the start to make the next 8 areas of the home flow better.

Chapter 6
The Journey

Now that you have the center of your home balanced, are you feeling healthy, balanced and ready to begin your journey? This is such an exciting area of the Ba Gua because we are starting something new. Activating this area of the home will certainly get things going. Are you doing what you love? Do you feel aligned with your life's purpose? When you try new things, what comes up for you? Do you feel that anything is possible for you? Do you believe you have unique gifts to contribute during your life experience? Do you take time to rest after finishing one project before beginning a new one?

The journey area is also referred to as the career area. This is a limited English translation. A closer translation would be "life path," since it refers more to the alignment of the soul with a particular life journey than it does with a chosen profession. The journey area is the beginning point of each new journey, decision, or life cycle. It represents the womb, the gestation period, and merging with universal consciousness. Associated with the water element, it represents the great mother from which all life springs. This is a state of complete merging; where one's individual personality (ego) disappears. Once merged with the infinite, everything becomes possible. It is from this realm of infinite possibilities that new beginnings open up.

Before we can begin our new journey, we need to examine what we believe. Did you know that we limit our potential because of beliefs that we have. We are limited because of our beliefs about reality, not reality itself. Many of these beliefs have been passed down to us, and passed down as truth; so we made an *agreement* (of *the four agreements*) that these beliefs were truth. If we can find the courage to be wrong about these beliefs or limiting perspectives, we open ourselves up to new possibilities; endless possibilities.

I challenge you to give yourself permission to be wrong. Instead of buying into limiting beliefs, buy into maybe: Maybe I'm smart enough to go back to school; Maybe I can get that promotion; Maybe I can be wealthy; Maybe my marriage can work out. You fill in the blanks after the word *maybe*. Maybe this will be the time in your life that you will have the courage to release all limiting beliefs you bought as truth and find your authentic self and live your authentic life.

Whatever it is you ask for is what you will receive. This keeps some people from asking, because the unknown is scary. Remember growing up when our parents used to tell us that being a kid was the fun time of life? That being the grown up was hard? Paying the bills, going to work, dealing with adult life was hard? They were misinformed. Life isn't supposed to be hard; life is supposed to be fun. When I look at our children, I think wow they are having a fun childhood, and I also think about the incredible adult life they will have. Unlimited potential, they can do anything they want with their life. It was through the process of admiring our children that I thought about me. I began to see me in them. It occurred to me that if they could do anything they wanted to with their life, than maybe I could too. From that one thought, came hundreds more. I just focus on doing what I love and more of those thoughts come. I had to look at what I had believed in the past and why I believed it; and then I got to release what wasn't working for me, what was limiting me.

What can being wrong mean? It can mean that you really are capable of making your dreams come true. Sometimes we don't meet the exact goal we were shooting for, but something more beautiful than we imagined comes out of it and if we hadn't tried something, we would have nothing. Listen to your inner voice that is guiding you through this journey, the journey is much more fun. When we listen and follow our spirit, it doesn't matter if we win or lose; we are enjoying the ride. We understand that we are learning and growing in every moment, and it feels right.

Place a water element somewhere in this space. Have the water running toward the door if you are putting this element outside. If it is a pond, you can add 8 black fish and one gold. Eight is for abundance, and the ninth is a tithe to the universe. If adding a water element isn't an option, use the list from the elements chapter to give you ideas on ways to create this in your space.

Activating the journey area of the home is key. This will begin a cycle that will change the direction of your life. You will have inspired ideas, and it is your job to act on them. You don't have to understand why you are acting; just know that you are preparing for change.

Two and a half years ago, we activated the journey area of our home. Within two weeks Paul came to me to talk about going back to school. He had chosen a BS in Business Management. He didn't have in mind anything specific he would do with this degree; he just knew that he needed it. Paul graduated in July 2006. In the time since he went back to school, we have started one business and bought another one. We see now why he needed a business management degree. At the time if he had decided not to go, he would be starting from square one and we wouldn't have the knowledge to run these businesses on our own. I am able to do what I love and let him do the part he loves. This is why it is so important to act on our thoughts, even when we don't know why. The source that we are coming from is us, and the more we begin to listen to ourselves the easier and more fun our journey will be.

You have a few choices here in the journey sector. If you know what it is that you want to do, ask for it, give thanks for it and keep doing the next thing until you find yourself there. Yes, it is that easy. It is like following a map to get to a certain destination. Know where you are going and plan it out step by step. Do the research of what needs to happen to get there. Plan it out and do one step at a time. When we break it up, it is more achievable and less stressful. When we finish one thing, we gain confidence to do the next thing and then the next and before we know it, we have arrived at our chosen destination. That is what this sector of the Ba Gua is all about.

The creative cycle of being on your path is exhilarating, you are balanced and energized and open to what if. Have fun working here. Give yourself time to clear this area out and get it activated. Come up with your own way of representing the water element here. The more meaning it has for you, the more powerful the adjustments will be.

Here are some questions to look at before working in the journey area of the home:

- Do you feel aligned with your life's purpose?
- When you try new things, what comes up for you?
- Do you feel that anything is possible for you?
- Do you believe you have unique gifts to contribute during your life experience?
- Do you take time to rest after finishing one project before beginning a new one?

As you get your journey area activated, you will find your answers to these questions come back as "Yes!" You will begin to try new things. Some will feel right and some won't. This will get you to the next place, so you will release the things that don't feel right. You will find the childlike faith that so many of us lost along the way. You will embrace your gifts, use them and watch yourself do things you never imagined were possible for you. You will allow yourself to rest, and will find that there is plenty of time in the day for all of the things that you need and want to get done. Have fun getting this area activated and have fun on your new journey.

Chapter 7
Self-knowledge / Wisdom

In the last chapter we worked on our journey area, aligning with our life path. We practiced being wrong about things we thought were true. What did you learn? This was an important process because in this chapter we will be moving into our self-knowledge or wisdom area.

The energy of self-knowledge is the process of seeing who we are and distinguishing the self from the watery abyss of the journey gua. Associated with the element of earth, this sector encourages the process of individuation. As the infant realizes he is separate from mother, individuation starts to occur. This process involves setting clear boundaries and distinguishing your needs from the needs of those around you. As the mountain, you must learn to be still, centered, grounded and feel your own strength.

This sector is concerned with the development of skills and knowledge necessary to achieve your chosen life path. This is about developing knowledge and wisdom. This is a great area of the home to read, study, meditate or pray. You can put items in three's such as pictures, or objects of people or even books written by people that you respect. This is not the place for pictures or items from people you don't want to gain knowledge from, such as people that have limited perspectives on life or that are not supportive of you on your life journey.

This is a place to get to know yourself, nurture yourself, and decide what you want to do; gain the knowledge to do it; and then watch it happen. I believe that specific goals are necessary. However, don't get so bogged down with what has to be that you miss what could be. When we are open to possibilities, the possibilities become endless. The universe is always sending us opportunities. Sometimes they come in a form we may perceive as tragedy or annoyance, or we just overlook it because it doesn't appear like we had envisioned. When we approach these situations with our eyes closed and our mind open, we are on our path and will be amazed at the opportunities that present themselves and the people that rush in to help us.

I challenge you to remember what your dreams were when you were a child. You didn't plan your career or life based on income; you based it on what you were passionate about. What are you passionate about now? How much different would your life be if you were on your path, living your dream and looking forward to doing what you do? Don't bring dollar signs into this, think about passion. You do your part, and the universe will come in and take care of the rest. Yes, it really is that easy. It's trusting that you will be taken care of; guided through this journey. Trust yourself and your dream enough to bring it to life.

The element in this area is earth. Remember that fire replenishes earth; so fire works here. Make this area earthy and grounding; supporting you while you are studying and learning about yourself and your journey. You will begin to notice changes in yourself when you get this area activated. You will begin to see clearer boundaries; how you are separate from others and how it is not your responsibility to make others happy or to take care of others at the cost of you. It isn't that you aren't compassionate, caring and giving; but you will have the wisdom to know what is healthy and what isn't and you will begin to take care of yourself so that you can take care of others. Sometimes taking care of others means showing them that they can take care of themselves.

The color for this area is blue, and the shape is square. Reds work well here along with any fire element such as actual candles or even a fireplace. Wood doesn't work well here since wood breaks up the earth.

When looking at self knowledge, here are some questions to ask yourself:

- How much time do you spend alone?
- What kinds of things do you like to do by yourself?
- Are you afraid to be alone?
- Do you feel like there's enough time, money, or energy for you?
- When you get extra time or money, what do you spend it on?

- Do you feel that your boundaries are clearly defined? Do others often overstep?

We don't need to be told how to behave, believe, or treat others. We just know. We have blocked out so much of our wisdom, and activating this sector of our home is a way to help us remember. Start paying attention to what you know, and tap into it. Have fun and be easy on yourself. Have fun dreaming and bringing those dreams to life. Life is short. DREAM BIG!! What is there to lose?

Chapter 8
Ancestry

Did you have fun dreaming? Did you dream big? Working with the energy of self-knowledge is a fun one. We begin to realize how many opportunities are sent our way and how we judge them instead of just being grateful. We are where we are because this is what we chose. Sometimes we chose these paths because we needed to wake up, get out of the fog or even let go of limiting beliefs. When we wake up and say this isn't what I choose anymore; we have the power to change it. We just have to choose another opportunity. This is about being on our path.

Now that you have found yourself in the self-knowledge area, the family area helps you discover who you are within the context of your family. This area is about all those that came before you and made it possible for you to be here. It provides you opportunity for continued growth. It is the foundation of individual growth.

This can be a tough one, especially if your family of origin isn't especially in favor of your life path. If you come from a family that has limited beliefs, and you are ready to let go of the limiting beliefs; it is important to make sure that you have activated the self-knowledge Gua, and found yourself and accepted yourself. You don't want to be carrying around their "stuff."

While preparing for my monthly newsletter about the family / ancestry area of the home, I decided to work in that area of our home. I thought about those that came before me, and what they left behind. This prompted me to think about the kind of person I want to be, the kind of parent I want to be and the kind of legacy I want to leave. In one of my favorite books, *Life Cycles*, Christine DeLorey describes this perfectly:

Special understanding and attention should now be given to children. Parents often feel overwhelmed by their responsibility to raise their offspring in safety and can often lay down the law without realizing that children must also have freedom. It is damaging to expect too much or too little from them. It is destructive to focus only on their negative traits while ignoring their real talents and their loving attributes. In today's evolving and dangerous world, young people need inclusion, love, understanding and, above all, encouragement. They need to know that life is not a series of punishments; but, rather, it is a series of consequences.

For every action there is a reaction. For every cause there is an effect. Peer pressure must be shown for what it is: just part of the big "race," the massive competition between human beings that is now very out of place on this planet. Children must be free to express their feelings, and their feelings must be accepted as part of their individuality. If they are encouraged to follow their hearts' desires–their free will--while allowing others the same freedom, they will seldom go wrong. Of course that applies to all of us. This is the perfect time to learn the difference between helping and interfering; loving and controlling; accepting and denying. Wherever there is judgment, guilt, or control; love cannot survive.

Working in the family area is tough; you find things that were lost. Sometimes you wish they would stay lost, but this gives you a greater understanding of who you are and who you are not. I had a beautiful experience with finding myself. I had been told I was a lot of things growing up, but this process led me to find the real me--not the perceptions that were thrown on me by the adults in my life. It gave me reason to dig in deep, to see what else had been lost. This wasn't a time for self pity, anger or blame; it was a time for celebration. I began to realize that I was strong and could literally do anything I wanted to with my life I could really have the family that I had always wanted; and I did.

I began to realize that I am married to a great man and we have great children. We understand each other, respect each other, talk to each other and apologize when we mess up. We must realize that we all have the right to learn and grow; and when you learn and grow sometimes you fall, and have to get back up. Does falling mean failure? It only means failure when you don't get back up. We are here to teach, to learn and to grow. Sometimes we get to teach our children, sometimes they get to teach us. When there is no judgment about it, it is beautiful and the lesson is more meaningful.

Does this mean that life is perfect all of the time? Yes, it does, when we don't have to make judgments about everything, and can just enjoy life and learn lessons when we need to. If we get what we focus on and we expect it to be a certain way, then it will always be that way. The thing I would like you to keep in mind is that if things aren't working out the way you intended, you need to go back and intend the outcome you want. Take all the judgment out of what is happening and enjoy life. Sometimes we just have to trust (not that it isn't scary). Remember faith is required!

What limiting beliefs do you have that you are ready to release?

- I'm not pretty enough, good enough, smart enough....
- I have to lie about who I am or I won't be accepted....
- I have to make others wrong so that I can be right....
- I have to struggle; it is a part of life....

Let them go. They are lies! You have the power to do anything that you want with your life. When you look at your children; see yourself. Talk to yourself with the same encouragement you talk to them with. You want to have that same love for yourself that you have for your children. No more having to live through them. Live life yourself! You don't have to be upset by a choice that they have made. It isn't your life. Live your life with open arms, and your children will follow suit. They won't have to rebel. They will have the freedom they want; the freedom they need.

Now is your chance. Write down what you are going to let go of. What are you going to keep? Take some time and put it on paper. You will feel better, and it will become clearer for you.

Cherished Beliefs	Limiting Beliefs

The family area of the home needs to be clutter free and organized. If you have to hire a professional, then do it. Nothing should be hidden, unless family secrets are what you want to keep experiencing. By this, I mean instead of cleaning up, you just throw things in drawers and places to keep them from sight, knowing all the time that they are there. If you are keeping this area cluttered, you are holding onto old family patterns, releasing the clutter will help you in releasing the patterns. Are you really ready for change?

Use the following questions to evaluate the status of your Family Heritage sector:

Do you have a tendency to hold onto things from the past that serve no purpose now?

Are you the storekeeper of the family heirlooms?

Do you display photographs of family members?

Are there any members missing from your photo collection?

Are there objects in your home that remind you of where you grew up?

How do you feel about those objects?

Have you kept things that your parents gave you?

Green is the color you are looking for here and yin wood, or wide stripes. You can achieve this with art, paint or objects. Picture a wide vertical stripe. Now see this as a book case, a dining room table, and curtains. Get the idea? Don't want to paint the room green? Have something green in the room. Stay away from white, fire and metal. (Remember the elements chapter?) Are you seeing the pattern? Are you getting creative? Make this about you, about your family and about your creation. You can create it anyway you would like!

Chapter 9
Abundance

Caution If you haven't worked on the center of your home, go back to Chapter 6 and get the center of your home balanced. If the center isn't balanced, you won't make any lasting changes.

What did you learn from your family in the last chapter? What did you find that you forgot was there? How did your focus change? What did you realize that you could let go of? What did your realize you could hold dear? Isn't it interesting how we limit our potential based on others' opinions? Isn't our capacity to love, create and accept in all of us? If you are holding onto limiting beliefs about abundance you will block the flow of it, no matter how much you want it. If your home contradicts what you are trying to create, it won't manifest. In the same respect, if your beliefs contradict what you are trying to create and your home is trying to bring it in, it won't show up. Sounds like too much work? It's not, you just need to release the junk you have picked up along the way and decide what it is that you want to bring in. Then, watch it flow! This is about visualization, expectation and faith!

As the branches of a tree receive the movement of the wind, this sector represents your ability to open to and receive the bounties of the universe. If you've ever had a day when you were doing what you absolutely loved, and ended the day feeling more energized than you began, you've experienced this energy pattern. Abundance energy encourages us to be more fully ourselves, to live our dreams and give our gifts. This Gua is often associated with material wealth, and it's true that money can greatly facilitate the pursuit of dreams. However, focusing on money often prevents us from seeing the abundance that is present all around us. By acknowledging the numerous manifestations of abundance, our relationship with money often changes as well. The element wood governs this Gua. The color is purple or jewel tones, and the shape is vertical rectangle.

Don't fool yourself. Activating this sector will boost up your cash, but it won't fix an underlying problem. If you are boosting this area up to fix a financial situation, it will bring to the surface your issue with money and why you either attract or repel it. Sometimes this can be a problem in your home (a fireplace in the wealth area) or a problem in your body (feelings of unworthiness). Both need to be addressed.

Activating this area will expose all of the abundance in your life. You will be amazed at the things drawn to your home, from stray animals to all forms of nature, to friends and even opportunity! Start giving thanks for all the forms of abundance that show up and you will attract more things to be grateful for. In your gratitude journal, write about the numerous ways that abundance shows up for you. Create it! Remember, the things you are giving thanks for don't need to be there yet. Giving thanks will bring them to you.

The abundance area of the home is about extravagance, wealth and royalty. The actual colors for this sector is purple, but if this doesn't fit your décor, get creative.

Thin vertical stripes (yang wood) in this area would be great, a water element to feed the wood or even an actual tree in this space; all of these are great choices to activate this sector. What resonates with you? What says wealth and extravagance to you? You really want to feel it, so that you can see it and then it will show up. You can even take the information that you have learned to find an adjustment that feels right to you--a customized adjustment. The power that this brings is actually more effective than others.

If your fireplace falls in this area of the home, you will have the same experience as you did if the sector were missing. A lack of energy in personal abundance and wealth results in the feeling that there is not enough. Not enough time. Not enough money. Not enough energy. It's as if the person has been cut off from the source and life dries up, feels blasé. Activities tend to tire more than excite or rejuvenate. Money is spent fixing problems (leaky faucet, medical bills, credit cards) more than enjoying life. It feels too risky to do something one really enjoys because of an ever-present fear that life will snatch enjoyment away, like a parent snatching candy away from a child.

If you haven't moved into or purchased this home, I would strongly advise against it. I have personally lived in this energy pattern, and although I'm grateful for the experience, I wouldn't recommend that you knowingly go there.

If you find yourself in this place, place a large mirror above the fire place, to symbolically put out the fire. Place a plant in front of the fire place and try to make the fireplace blend in as much as possible. Please, no bright fiery colors--especially red! Once your cures are in place, keep an eye on your financial situation, but don't come from a place of lack, come from a place of hopefulness.

Coming from fear will only cause the cures not to work, because you won't be expecting them to. When we get into these energy patterns of not having enough, we are focused on all of the things we can't buy, pay for or afford. The problem is that when this is our focus, we have more things we can't afford, we don't have enough money to pay our bills and we get into a deep, dark hole. The phrase the rich get richer and the poor get poorer is true. The reason it is true is because of our focus. Once we decide that we can't live like that any longer and shift our focus, we begin to see the flow shift. Try it for yourself, and see the manifestation powers that you have. Start with small things if you want, but try it and get in touch with the power that you have to create the life you want. Until internal and external issues have been addressed, the abundance won't flow; so stay in a place of gratitude.

Use the following questions to evaluate the status of your Abundance sector:

What is your financial situation?

Are you happy with it?

If not, where would you like it to be?

Do you make, but also spend a lot of money?

Is there not enough to start with?

Is there enough for what you want to do?

Are you passionate about what you do every day?

What are the areas of your life in which you feel abundant?

So your job is to go through this area of your home, clearing out any and all clutter, cleaning and giving it the respect it deserves. If there is anything blocking the flow of abundance, get rid of it; including those limiting beliefs. (Did you release those in the last chapter?) Begin to acknowledge all of the abundance flowing to you. I challenge you to get specific on what you want to draw into your life, and look for the courage to accept what you create with your eyes closed and your mind open!

Chapter 10
Fame / Reputation

In the last chapter we worked with the abundance area of the home. We looked for different ways that we are abundant. What are you abundant in? What are you drawing to you? An abundance of time, friends, love, opportunity, money? When we focus on what we have instead of what we don't have, it feels better, and we are more likely to invite things we love into our life. We create what we focus on, and if you focus on lack, that is what you will experience. If you focus on judgment and hate, this is what you experience. If you focus on love, forgiveness and understanding, this is what you will experience. Your world is a mirror; what do you see?

As we give our gifts fully and joyfully to the world, the world recognizes our accomplishments and efforts. This sector is your fame area, the place where you shine. It represents how you want to be recognized for what you spend your life's energy doing. It also gives the world a way to say thank you and to affirm that what you're doing with your life is valuable. This recognition is not always in the form of certificates or awards. It can be heart-felt thank you cards from friends or drawings from children, just as long as it expresses appreciation. The fame sector is governed by the fire element. You can create this by adding red or fiery paint, candles or even triangles. Get creative and don't forget to add those affirmations. Get specific on what you want to be known for, if your goals change, then change your affirmations.

As we move into the fame sector of the home, let's look at it from more of a reputation point of view than "being famous". Our reputation goes everywhere with us. It will help us get a job, friends and even opportunities. What do you want to be known for? What if you have made mistakes (like everyone else!) and you feel that your reputation is tarnished? Everybody loves a comeback story, if you have made mistakes in your past, don't fret, just realize it is a learning experience.

Some of us have been taught to come from fear. When we mess up, we have to be punished for a specific time period, or worse, forever. We are taught to overcompensate and go to the other extreme. Let's think about balance, about learning and growing, about forgiveness for ourselves and for others, and about finding our authentic self. The first step is to stop judging yourself (forgiveness). Hold your head up, and decide how you want to re-create yourself. In life, we are always teaching or learning. Learn the lesson, and let it go! When we come from authenticity, it shows.

Have you ever been around someone and felt like you couldn't be yourself. You acted in a way that wasn't you, to get their approval? Chances are they didn't like that version of you. They knew you were lying about something, and the truth was, you *were* lying! You were lying about who you are. When we come from authenticity, it doesn't matter if someone likes us or not, because we know who we are and that their feelings aren't about us anyway. Their feelings are a mirror for them. So now I challenge you, if you are ready, to pull out the authentic you. Notice how everything shifts when you are being you and loving it. Notice how people accept you, how they rush in to help you. Set the intention to find, accept and be your authentic self. Remember, we move into relationships next, if you are not being authentic, you will draw different people to you than if you are simply being you. Have fun accepting, loving and being you!

When working with clients, I have noticed a pattern. We are very hard on ourselves. We let moments define us, instead of looking at the big picture. This really isn't fair, because chances are, we don't hold others to that same standard. In the grand scheme of things do our life lessons really matter to everyone? Aren't we allowed to live our life, learn from our mistakes and make our life better? Don't we encourage others to do this? Shouldn't we allow ourselves the same acceptance?

Paul and I have a beautiful looking patchwork quilt framed in a shadow box. When I saw it, I was drawn to it. I called Paul to tell him I loved it and to see if he objected to me purchasing it without him seeing it. He told me to go ahead and pay for it, and he would pick it up on his way home, since it wouldn't fit in my car. He brought it in and put it on the wall and we were admiring it. I was showing him all of the parts of the quilt I loved, and then I said, "Well, I don't like this part or this part, but when you put it all together it is beautiful."

Paul said, "Yes, it is like our life. We have beautiful moments and dark moments; but when you look at our life as a whole, you see beauty."

Every time I look at that piece of art *and* every time we hit a bump in the road, I remember that conversation. Life is beautiful, lessons and all. I encourage you all to look at your life for a moment and enjoy the beauty you see.

Use the following questions to evaluate the status of your External Recognition sector:

What would you like someone to recognize you for?

How would they show they value you?

Is there anyone in your life that fully sees and appreciates what you do?

Do you feel visible?

Do you feel like you have something valuable to offer the world?

So how should we activate this sector of the home? This is a fire sector, the shape is triangle and the color is red. Painting a wall red in this area will call you forth, no doubt; but what if you don't like red? Let's think creatively for a moment. First, find something that you want to be known for, when I say something I'm talking about a piece of art, a book, thank you notes or something that gives you the feeling that you want to experience in regard to your reputation. Keep a red envelope with thank you notes, hang your diplomas or awards, have triangular curtains on windows or any color that is fiery. Keep the water and metal out of this area, but you can boost the fire by adding wood. If your fire place falls in this area, that is perfect; but please don't put a mirror above it (mirror = water). Instead, place a beautiful piece of art that inspires you to grow!

Chapter 11
Relationships

In this chapter, we are moving into the relationship area of the home. If you are looking to create or enhance a relationship or relationships, this is the place! Ruled by the earth element, this area of your home is dedicated to your connection with mother earth and other members of the human race. It represents your ability to make a commitment to something outside yourself; a career, a home or another person. After reaching your personal zenith (fame), you move into the interpersonal side of the Ba Gua cycle. It is related to the earth and encourages you to develop relationships of trust, intimacy and openness. To do this you must focus on trust, intimacy and openness.

This is not a place to go back to childhood and focus on unpleasant memories. What you focus on is what you create, if you don't want to re-create your childhood with your children, or spouse; focus on what kind of parent you want to be, what kind of spouse you want to be, what kind of person you want to be. Focusing on the negative will only encourage repetition.

This area of the home should have things in pairs and should be earthy and nurturing. This is ideal for the master bedroom or a social room, but isn't a good choice for a child's bedroom. If this is your bedroom, it's a fun room to decorate. You can put the "feel" you want in your relationship in this room and voila, you create that in your relationship (passion, closeness etc)! Keep peach out of your bedroom, as it encourages change, and please don't use triangles, unless you want to invite a third side into your relationship. Paint this room and spend time in here together, talking about hopes and dreams for your future! You create your reality, so why not create it together? Also remember that the first thing you see when you wake up is your perspective for the day. I recommend finding something that you both see in the morning so that you come from the same perspective. This should feel good to you--not a pile of laundry that needs folding, but something that encourages you to do your life's work; enjoy your relationship. It should be something inspiring.

If you are just beginning your Feng Shui journey, please don't start with this area of your home. It is tempting to want a relationship and think that the relationship will "complete" you. However, if you aren't balanced inside your home and your body, and you invite a relationship into your life; you will invite the one that resonates with you at this moment. As you begin to learn and grow, you will outgrow this relationship, which can result in pain. If this is something you want to create, it will just be a life lesson.

Be patient and find your balance instead of forcing something before the time is right! As you begin to shift, so will the relationships in your life. You will notice how different people show up; people that are more like you. This is support for you, welcome it! Enjoy working in this area of your home and creating your relationships!

As I began moving into relationships, I took inventory of this area of our home. What have Paul and I created together? What would I change? What kind of relationship do we have with our children? What would I change about it and what would they change about it? I have noticed how the tone I use when talking to them sets us up to work together or start a war. We create so much with our words, and the way we talk to each other builds us up or tears us down. How do I want my children to talk to others? Do I want them to just listen and follow without asking questions and exploring, or do I want them to think for themselves, educate themselves and trust themselves enough to make a decision based on what they feel about something?

I want to create authenticity in our family. You can tell what a person feels like inside by the way they act. When someone is comfortable in his or her skin, others are comfortable around them. They feel they have permission to be comfortable in their skin. This goes back to being authentic. When we are being authentic (ourselves) is when we look our best, feel our best, and become our best. It isn't a mask, hiding us from the world; it's showing ourselves to the world.

This is so incredible to me, because if telling myself I'm something different can make me behave different, this means I can tell myself anything I want to do or be. I realized that we could tell our children anything about themselves and they would believe us (telling them something negative once was like telling them something negative every day). So that finding the best in them, and showing that to them would be the way to show them who they are and who they can be. We are what we believe we are. What do you believe you are? How do you know that you are right? What if you were being just a small percentage of what you are? Here's to "what if."

I want you to stop here and look at the relationships that you currently have. Are they what you want or are they draining? Don't throw them away just yet. Instead I want you to fill the next 9 lines with how you would love your relationships to be. There is to be nothing negative here, only positive. We are in the process of creating, so have fun and make it good. Remember "the universe corresponds to the nature of your song" (Beckwith, 2006). What do you want the universe to correspond to in regard to your relationships? If you expect that you will have pleasant experiences with those around you, this is what you will get; let's get it in writing:

1. _____
2. _____
3. _____
4. _____
5. _____
6. _____
7. _____
8. _____
9. _____

How does that feel? When we have a belief about how our relationships are supposed to be, then this is what we will experience. So it is important to make sure we are clear on what we want to experience. You might put this list in your gratitude journal, read it often and feel it. This visualization is key in the creation process.

So the element in this sector is earth, the color is pink and the shape is a square. Did I lose you with the pink room? No worries, find an earthy color (any color that is muddy) a fleshy tone would be a great choice. You want it to have a nice reflection on your skin if this is your bedroom. Whatever room this is, paint it, spend time in here and try not to have this as a spare bedroom. This area should be grounding and should give you support. You also should spend time here to activate this area with your energy.

Use the following questions to evaluate the status of your Intimate Relations sector:

Are you in an intimate relationship?

If so, are you happy in that relationship?

If you're single, do you have an active social life with opportunities to connect with the type of people you enjoy?

How do you feel about your relationship with mother earth?

Have you incorporated patterns into your life that support and nurture the earth; such as recycling, composting, minimal waste, sustainable living, etc?

Do you feel connected to something larger than yourself?

When you make a commitment to a person or a project, do you follow through with it?

Have fun here, this will encourage fun in your relationships. Don't hide things here or have clutter. You don't want that in your relationships. Get this place in order, and watch the shift in your relationships.

Chapter 12
Creativity / Children

As we move into the children / creativity area of our home, we are encouraged to create and re-create until we get it right. The natural result of receiving the supportive and nurturing energy of the relationship area is a burst of creative energy. Sometimes this energy manifests in the birth of children; sometimes in other creative undertakings. This is the playground of life. You may have children who need a space where it's okay to play, explore, and create; and a place to destroy those creations. Regardless, you need that type of space yourself. A place where you don't take yourself or the world too seriously--a place to mess around, try things out and start over if you don't like it. This sector is also related to the metal element with pastels representing the color and as such is concerned with the creation of new things, especially intellectual ideas. This area can also be thought of as your goals, your vision and your future! No matter where this space is located in your home, activating this sector will benefit everyone in the home. Try to keep the fire element out of this area, unless you find that you are too rigid. Keep in mind that balance is key.

This is a place where we find the child in us, and how fun it is to have childlike faith! We can do anything we want with our lives; be and do anything we want. The key is *movement*. If we sit and *think* about it all of the time, we aren't *creating* it. It's time to get up and start fumbling our way through. It's okay for our goals to change as we grow; this is part of learning. Taking yourself too seriously here will result in stagnation and rigidness. Time goes quickly, so why wait any longer. What mark do you want to leave on this earth? You get to decide this and you also get to change your mind. The key is to have fun!

So many of us come up with "resolutions" that we think will make us happy: losing weight, making more money, etc. But these aren't the things that will truly make us happy. Being on our path, using our gifts and taking care of ourselves will! We all have our own special unique gifts to contribute. When we don't know what our gifts are, we might try to use someone else's and ours are wasted. What are your authentic gifts? This isn't a time to compare yourself to anyone; it is about looking inside and finding *your* way. This is the perfect time to look at what you want to create and start the process.

Do you want to lose some weight, create an unrealistic schedule for the family, or try to be someone you're not to gain approval from others? No thanks, instead, why not dig in deep and see who you are.

I was reading in my *Life Cycles* book, by Christine Delorey. She has such an amazing way with words. I read this sentence, and it hit home. "*Emptiness is your own sad and unfulfilled potential*" Oh my, how many times have I felt this emptiness. How many clients express this to me? How many people are out there in the world trying to cope with life--feeling empty and trying to cover it or ignore it? How many of us fill ourselves with numbing agents to avoid dealing with it? What if we all realized that this feeling is a form of *hell*, our own wisdom screaming out to us to do something different, to listen to ourselves and live up to our potential? What if we realized that listening to it and letting it guide us would remove this feeling and make our lives better than we could imagine? When we are in tune with our own unique wisdom, we are open to infinite possibilities and we are fulfilled. I challenge you to listen today; you will be amazed at what you will hear.

Use the following questions to evaluate the status of your Creative Offspring sector:

Do you generally feel excited about life?

Are you full of curiosity and wonder?

Do you make time to play and relax?

Do you enjoy your free time?

If you have children, are they imaginative in their play and positive in their outlook?

How do you express your creative energy?

This area is a metal sector, the colors are rainbow colors (pastels) and the shape is a circle. This is a great area for an office if you are trying to be creative. Whether *you* want the creative energy, your children need it or the whole family needs it; activating the creative offspring area of the home will benefit everyone. Have fun in this space, and let the décor show this freedom.

Chapter 13

Helpful People and Travel

We have been creative: birthing new ideas, dreams and goals. Now we need our "helpful people" to assist us in bringing them to fruition. It's a great time to recognize that we are all in this together; we can build each other up or tear each other down; what we give we will receive; and we create our own reality. The beauty of this is that if we don't like what we see, we just need to re-create it.

Once you have *clearly* defined your goals; activated your helpful people sector; and opened yourself to how helpful people will help you (and who those helpful people will be); you will begin to see your ideas, dreams, and goals become a reality.

Governed by the metal element, this sector helps you draw together the various pieces of your life's story and forge a chalice into which you pour all that you have learned and become along the way. This chalice is your ability to give and receive aid from others.

When you want to receive something, the best way to receive it is first to give it. If you find yourself short on cash, find a charity to donate to. Send them what you can, and watch it come back 10-fold. If you need helpful people to promote your business; promote someone else's. The energy you send to the universe is sent back to you multiplied. If you need love, encouragement, acceptance, forgiveness or even time; give these gifts and watch them come back to you. It is a predictable and incredible pattern. Remember, your world is a mirror. What do you see?

Use the following questions to evaluate the status of your Benefactors Sector:

Can you name five people who function as benefactors, teachers, or mentors in your life?

Are you currently functioning as a mentor to someone?

How do you feel in that role?

How often do you extend yourself beyond your spouse or family?

What communities do you participate in?

Common interest groups?

Religious groups?

Women's or men's groups?

Political associations?

Business associations?

Recreation or travel groups?

If you were to open more fully to a sense of community, what type of people would you want to spend more time with?

This area of your home is also strongly tied to travel; especially in retirement years. Regardless of where you are on your journey, this is a great place for maps, globes or Angels. Our son, Logan, occupies this space of our home. We have decorated his room with airplanes and maps. At age nine, he wants to connect with the maps, so we have decided to put a specific laminated map only for him to use for vacation destinations. He can mark the spot where he wants to go and write about when and why he wants to go. Remember that including family members in the creative process will help with the manifestation process. Also, remember that we get what we expect!

If maps, globes, or pictures of globes aren't an option, and you are in need of helpful, consider placing these items behind existing pictures. Get creative in finding ways to identify your territory. You can also place items in this area that represent or mean the same thing to you. Remember that the more creative and meaningful your adjustment is to you, the more powerful it will be.

Hang a wind chime on this corner of the house. The sound energy will "call in" these helpful people. The colors here are grey and white, and the element is metal. The shape of a circle works well here, but you want to avoid fire.

Chapter 14
Limiting Beliefs and Balance

As you begin and continue to work in your home; keep in mind that the limiting beliefs we hold onto actually create imbalances in our home, our bodies and our lives. We can be so shortsighted and not see that things in moderation are better than things withheld or in excess. We can fail to enjoy the simple things in life because of limiting beliefs. As you begin to activate your home, try first for balance. Watch how you change, how you connect with yourself for the first time. Opportunities will present themselves to you, and you will find that you have more choices than you ever knew. As you make judgments about things, ask why you are judging it? Where did you get your information? Have you asked yourself? Start asking yourself. Give yourself permission to enjoy life and enjoy the balance that you will create from not depriving yourself of things you love or overindulging in things you love. Remember *balance*.

We have so many distractions in life: expectations about what we need to do, be or have to be happy.

Sometimes we get confused by all of the contradictions that are implied. We have an underlying belief that money is bad, but that if we have it we will be more accepted. So then we are torn because we want nice things but then have the guilt over it. As if that whole contradiction isn't bad enough, we also have a belief that we have to look perfect. Then we realize that we can never look perfect, and so we begin to believe that we would be happier if we were thinner, prettier, didn't have freckles, stretch marks or wrinkles. All of these distractions keep us from living in the moment and enjoying our beautiful life. We have bought into the lie that external factors determine our happiness. It isn't just as children and teenagers; we carry this into adulthood; until death do we part from these silly limiting beliefs.

One ingredient for a happy life is acceptance: of yourself, others and of where you are right now. It is about being who you authentically are, and not changing to please others. Once we begin to acknowledge who we are, we will attract and develop more relationships that will support us. We will teach this to our children and they will begin to pass this down to their children (instead of the contradictions that have been passed down in the past). Acceptance is contagious; and when we accept ourselves, we begin to accept others. Seeing the best in yourself, gives you the freedom to see the best in others. If you are allowed to be different, you will celebrate others' differences. It is freeing!

Trust is another key ingredient for a happy life. Once we trust that we are in the right place at the right time and that people are there to help us; this is what we will attract. We will attract a path that will give us everything we need to make our dreams a reality. This power of knowing that everything aligns for you is crucial. It eliminates the fears that we have. We no longer say, "Oh no, how are we going to do this or that?" It is just exciting to see how it will show up.
(*The Secret*, 2006) What we think about we bring about, so trust and you will attract to you events that will give you reason to trust.

Living your life on purpose is another key to happiness. Decide the experiences that you want to experience; and experience them. If you get there and decide it isn't your path; change paths. Too many times we believe, "Well I made this bed, and so now I must lie in it." How ridiculous is this belief? This is how we learn and grow; how we get to know who we are and who we are not. Let's stop taking ourselves so seriously and have fun with life. I would be sad for my children if they played it safe, and punished themselves instead of learning and growing from mistakes. We can do anything we want with our life; why do we not enjoy it?

Imagine the world that we would live in if we would wake up and realize that happiness doesn't have anything to do with external factors. Happiness is about what is in us. When we realize that it is all about what we focus on, and then we embrace our authentic self and live our dream; we will be happy beyond belief. We must realize that money doesn't make us *bad* or fulfill our dreams; we do that ourselves. Money and appearance don't define us and our happiness; we define us and our happiness.

For a minute I would like you to imagine that you can do anything with your life. Be quiet for a minute and think, "If I could do anything with my life, what would it be?" Don't think about the how, just imagine the end result. What moves you? What inspires you? Whatever it is you want to be, you can. Right now, stop buying into the opinion that it's too hard, ask for the way and you will find it. Some people say "I want to change my life, make change, but I'm too tired, sick or afraid. I can't, I can't, I can't." If this comes out of your mouth, I am telling you that you don't want your life to change and that you are making excuses. I'm not trying to be harsh, but the truth is that you can or can't do whatever it is that you believe. Once you realize that you have the power to create anything you want and start creating on purpose, you will realize what a remarkable person you are and the silly worries will fall away. If you create the opportunity to do something with your life that feels good on a soul level, is the superficial nonsense we focus on really going to matter?

We pick up limiting beliefs all around us. As children, we get them from our parents and then we take them and share them. We put limits on everything that we do. Limiting beliefs are *anything* that put limits on us. What is the first thing you notice about someone when you meet them? You notice how you feel around them. Many times when we meet someone we say, "She is so pretty." What this usually means is, "I liked the way I felt when I was around her." What is pretty anyway? Is it superficial? Aren't looking pretty and being pretty two completely different things? Why do we make ourselves less because of the size our clothes or how many wrinkles are on our face? We are limiting our potential based on a natural aging process or, worse yet, what God gave us!

We need to get very in tune with our reactions to people. This reaction should not be based on appearance, but rather the energy of the person. Sometimes we can miss out on something very special because it isn't packaged in the manner we think it should be. We can also experience pain for the very same, but opposite reason; by not listening to ourselves because a person looks like something they are not. Begin to pay attention. It is in all of us, we have just chosen to ignore it. What if we tried living with our eyes shut and our mind open?

When I was in elementary school, someone told me that my legs were fat. I don't remember if she was joking, teasing or actually serious. It doesn't matter really. What I took from that one comment was that my legs were fat and that was bad, and I should cover them up at all costs! I didn't wear skirts or dresses unless forced to do so, and people would ask me often why I didn't wear skirts. I never told them it was because my legs were fat. When I was in junior high I got this beautiful mini skirt for Christmas. It was the most beautiful skirt I'd ever seen and was certainly hip. I thought that if I wore black hose with it, it would slim my "fat" legs. So I tried it, with a sick stomach and a lot of fear. What was the most interesting thing that happened was that all I heard from the guys and the girls were how beautiful my legs were, and why didn't I ever wear skirts! I have no idea whether my legs are fat or beautiful, but my opinion is that they are my best feature and I love and take care of them because that opinion of me just feels better.

As simple an example of limiting beliefs this is, it is in fact a limiting belief. I had listened to someone else's opinion of me instead of finding out for myself. I can look at the pattern of my life and see the same thing over and over. I spent so much time being the person that I was told I was, that I never actually knew who I was. I just kept being the person the people around me told me to be.

This is so key, so pay attention. This has taken me time, trial and error; but I have found that I am who I say that I am and this gives me unlimited potential. I can be anything I want, do anything I want. I have to clear my head sometimes when I hear the limiting beliefs that I used to believe. When those old thought patterns return, I have to remind myself that I CAN DO ANYTHING, and that those thoughts aren't mine-

-they don't belong to me. They are then free to leave, and I feel better.

If you look back at your life, you will see how you have drawn circumstances and opportunities to you. Think about how you just knew something would happen; and it did (good or bad things). The *knowing* you had in that moment attracted it to you. Try it with something little if you need to, but the fact of the matter is you can create it however you want. Enjoy this process of acceptance, of yourself and others. Trust yourself and others, and in this process you will find that you are living your life on purpose.

As your beliefs about yourself change; you release the limiting beliefs that you have, and your home will become in alignment with your beliefs and your dreams. You will see that you are creating your life on purpose. It is a beautiful process; enjoy it!

Closing thoughts...

Now that you have a new understanding of how your environment, your beliefs, and your attitude shape your life; what will you do with this information? You have been shown some new tools to adjust your life and create a purpose. I hope that you have fun with this, are gentle with yourself and embrace what you create.

If you have followed along in the online classroom, you have developed some good habits about journaling what you want to create and giving thanks for what you already have. I hope that you keep this up on your journey. When we hit bumps in the road, it is nice to be able to go back and get re-focused.

As you see your goals being achieved, I challenge you to make new ones and make adjustments accordingly. We have the student lounge (the forum) to visit and post questions in as they come up. Use this as your goals change if you need some direction.

www.thefengshuitrainingcenter.com/studentlounge

Blessings,
Leigh

Appendix A
Interesting Stories

The Wealth Corner – A particular home had a kitchen in the wealth corner of the home. We can look at the water in the kitchen as feeding the wood element, the stove is a little harder to get creative with. When I arrived, there were many issues to deal with; however at the time, money was a major one. I went through the home and the biggest obstacle they needed to deal with was clutter. Clutter everywhere, so much it was exhausting. I could see why money was so scarce; they weren't showing respect to what they owned. We activated the wealth area; and she cleaned it, organized it a bit and stopped there. The rest was just too overwhelming for her. Within a week, she received a sum of about $13,000 so that she could pay off her vehicle and save over $500 per month. This was a case of activating a sector and receiving a gift! However, the relationship with money didn't change because the family's relationship with money didn't change, and they ended up back in the same spot.

Moral, if you're trying to change something; go deep, so it will be lasting.

The Beautiful Rent Home – At one of the first homes I had done since my certification, the owners could barely pay the rent. They were living paycheck-to-paycheck and not very comfortable. I went through the home and cleared it out, spoke blessings and set some intentions. There were also things they needed to adjust. The interesting thing about this home was that there weren't glaring problems. There were minor things in the wealth, reputation and journey areas. The energy surrounding the home was what needed the most work. This couple had been through major debt problems and wanted desperately to get out from under the mess they had created. They were working on cleaning it up by paying it off and using their credit to their benefit. The husband wanted a different job, one that was making more money. I received a call from the wife about five months later. She wasn't feeling settled and wanted change. She just wasn't sure what change that was! I asked her to make a list of things that had shifted so she could see things more clearly. Once she put it on paper, she could see that everything she had asked for was there; she just hadn't taken the time to look. About one month later, I received an e-mail, asking if she could schedule a consultation on their new, 3000 sq ft home!!

The Cubicle – I received a call from a client, who had just been past over for a promotion. She had been with this large software company for over five years, and she had been working on the promotion for two. She decided to have me come out and "Feng Shui" her cube. Upon arrival, I noticed that it was cluttered and dusty. There were lots of family pictures in her wealth sector, and a few awards up in her relationship corner (some of her awards had been thrown in the trash!). She had detrimental energy patterns coming from a few "negative" neighbors, so we cleared them and asked for beneficial energy patterns to replace them. The cube not only looked different when I left, but felt so much lighter. She went on vacation for a week, and upon return from vacation, her boss called her in to tell her how impressed he was with her performance. Hum?????

The Bonsai – I was working out of an office holding workshops, and the energy moved very slowly. Not just for my workshops, but for the facility in general. After sitting and speaking with the owner and those that worked there, I asked if I could Feng Shui the space. The space was beautiful, every detail taken care of; however, the furniture density was too high and there were a lot of things that needed to be moved out. This was a case of less would be more. My biggest concern in this process was a bonsai plant in the center of the space. What it represented was this big beautiful tree, perfect in everything, except the fact that it had been dwarfed. It was contained. This bonsai plant was the center of everything. I told the owner my concern, and she said she had spent too much money on it to get rid of it--a grand total of $400. I asked her if $400 was worth losing her business over? She laughed and blew it off. I asked her to remove it from the center and place it somewhere else for a month to see what shifted. She refused. Three months later, they had to shut the doors! Over one million dollars in putting this place together went out the door. Point to this story: When you have a practitioner come into your home or office, listen to them! Try the recommendations, you don't have to leave it that way forever; just try it!

The "For Sale" Home - I got a phone call from a Realtor, asking for help with a home she had on the market for a year with no offers. I met her at the home and found that the home was so odd-shaped that it was missing the journey and self-knowledge Gua. The waterfall in the front was facing the street and when I entered the home, I felt a heaviness that made me want to cry. I could see that the occupants weren't on their life path, since it was missing completely from their home and that they had a hard time setting boundaries, finding their way, and confusing their responsibility with that of others. The adult daughter was living there, and occupying the relationship Gua of the space.

I cleared the space, and then symbolically stretched the home out to square it off so the missing sectors could be activated. Within a week, shifts were happening. The family was fighting. Were they waking up? Were they going to listen and get on path? Dad found a temp job. He had been unemployed for years; and only two weeks after my visit, the house was under contract. That is a lot of change in two weeks!

The Eight Thousand Dollars - I went to Feng Shui a home, gave recommendations and left. I received a phone call less than a week later to tell me that they were now broke!! What did I do???? I promptly went back to the house to check it out. Everything looked fine until I went into the master bedroom, which was also the wealth area. The client had moved her TV stand to form a triangle. This creates a fire element in a wood sector which results in the burning of money. I told her to put the TV up against the wall and that should fix the problem. I have to admit that she looked at me like I was from another planet, but she moved it. Within 2 days she had a small flow of cash come in (about $500) and within the week she FOUND $8000 she didn't know she had....

Appendix B
Feng Shui Q & A
With Leigh & Paul

Q: I keep some hunting rifles under my bed. Is it possible that this is contributing to my wife's inability to get a good night's sleep?

Bennie
Round Rock, Texas

A: Let me ask you this. Do guns make your wife nervous? Objects under our bed are linked to our personal chi. When we sleep, we are recharging ourselves and this should be done in the most comfortable, secure place in our home. This place should be our bed. If you are going to keep anything under your bed, it should be objects that will link your personal chi with your goals and desires. Keeping guns under the bed would not promote positive chi for most and this may be the reason your wife is having trouble sleeping. Put your guns in a safe with the ammo locked up separately. This will create a more secure environment for your wife and prevent any unfortunate accidents concerning your guns. Sweet dreams!

Happy New Year,
Paul

I just wanted to add something to Paul's answer. We placed a treasure box under our bed, and that is all we keep under there. I'm attaching ideas for a treasure box of your own! Whatever you place under your bed, directly beneath your person, is linked to your personal chi. The Chinese traditionally placed a bowl of rice under a woman to symbolically link her personal chi to the energy of fertility. Numerous Feng Shui rituals involve placing money under the bed to bond a person's chi with the energy of financial abundance. This area of your living space deserves careful consideration. When we sleep, we relax our physical, psychic, and emotional boundaries. Whatever energy is present during this sleep state will influence all our conscious moments. One of the most powerful ways to work with this space is to create a treasure box or a joy bowl:

Treasure Box or Joy Bowl

Choose a Container:

- A box has the energy of embracing and holding.
- A bowl has an open quality that invites something new in.
- The style, material and type of container affect its energy, which sets the vibration for the entire adjustment.
- For clarity, consider a clear glass bowl.
- For abundance, consider a box with ornate carving or a jewel studded cover.
- For strength and support, consider an earthen pottery bowl or a solid wooden box.
- For flexibility and flow, consider a woven basket or an abalone shell.

What to Include:

- When deciding what to put in the treasure box, think about what gives you joy. Don't only put money in the box unless that is all you want to create. You want a balanced treasure box since this encourages a balanced life.
- When placing money in the box, don't put change, or this is what you will attract. Try placing one bill of each denomination in the box: a one, five, ten, twenty, fifty and a hundred dollar bill representing willingness to manifest abundance on many levels.
- You can also write out a check for the amount that you need to receive in order for something to happen. Write an amount or more so you don't create unnecessary limitations.
- For abundance of time, include a watch. Make sure it is in good working order.
- If you want to be more flexible and understanding of others, include rubber bands.
- For more passion, place a container of massage oil, a favorite scent, or a picture of two people

enjoying each other with the kind of passion you want to experience.

- For inner peace and contentment, you can place a single candle, incense stick, or other meditative object in the box.
- To represent an increase of cooperation and good will, place two red strings tied with a square knot in the box. This represents the unification of disparate energies.
- Place a rainbow colored candle, or some other item with all seven-rainbow colors, to invite harmony and balance into your life.
- For an abundance of friends and helpful supporters, you can place anything circular in the box. For a more literal representation, you can use a ceramic candleholder that depicts a circle of friends holding hands.
- For an abundance of energy, place a spiral-shaped copper coil in the box. Copper is a strong energy activator and the spiral represents the spiraling coil of energy through the chakras.

Whatever you place in the box, make sure it has significance for you personally. You should spend a minute speaking out loud your desires for abundance and desires for your life. When you use your voice, it aligns your body and spirit with your actions and strengthens your intent. This is a fun one to do together! Enjoy!

Blessings,
~Leigh

Q. With the holidays upon us, I was wondering how hanging lights and decorations around the exterior of my house would affect my home from a Feng Shui perspective.

Telle
Apache Springs, New Mexico

A. Let me start off by asking you a question: What do the lights and decorations represent to you and your family? For me the holidays are a time of reflection, celebration, and togetherness. The lights and decorations for my family are part of the celebration of life, a sort of thanks to God for allowing us to enjoy all the pleasures he has given us. Ninety% of Feng Shui is intention, so in our case the intention is to enjoy the holidays and part of that celebration is through the beauty of lights, colors, and even sounds. The lights and decorations are a joyous element and that will attract positive chi, or energy, to your home. So decorate as brightly as you wish. This will not create any negative affects from a Feng Shui point of view. Just be sure to recognize your intentions.

Happy Holidays,
Paul

Q. I have been trying to get pregnant for almost a year, with no luck. I'm not ready to go to a specialist yet. Is there any Feng Shui cure to help me?

Nancy
Austin, Texas

A. I love transcendental cures!! Here is a conception cure. Have fun!! Place a small bowl of rice under the bed where the woman sleeps. Leave the bowl there for 27 days to absorb ling (one connected with or having the quality of) . Each night when the woman goes to sleep, she should visualize the ling entering the rice. On the 27th day, remove the rice and mix it with 151 proof alcohol, adding one drop for every year of the man's life and one drop for every year of the woman's, and adding an additional drop for the new life that's about to enter their home. Place the alcohol/rice mixture under the bed while the couple has intercourse. Remove the rice and bury it in the ground outside in the creative offspring area of the yard.

Good luck and have fun!!

Blessings,
~ Leigh

Q. I want to go in a different direction with my career, but I'm not sure where to start. From a Feng Shui point of view, where would I begin?

Lynda
Round Rock, Texas

A. This is a very common question, even when you aren't looking at it from a Feng Shui point of view. The most important thing I tell my clients is to get the center of the home balanced. This can be as simple as finding the exact center of the home and putting a circular piece of paper with affirmations about balance on it. The next step is to activate your journey sector. You can do this with a water feature. If you are on a tight budget, you can pick one up at Walgreen's for $5.99. Stop putting limits on yourself and practice being wrong. If you knew everything, you would be content in your career and a change wouldn't be desired. As you open up, so will the opportunities! Have fun learning and growing, this is a fun time!

Blessings,

Leigh

Q. I love to cook out in my backyard. From a Feng Shui perspective, is there any special place that I should keep my grill?

John
Lakeway, Texas

A. Great question. This is one that people tend to overlook. Your grill, whether it is gas, charcoal, or wood burning, represents the fire element. There are a couple of ways to look at this. There is a rule of thumb concerning patios and whether or not they are included in the Ba Gua of your home or of your yard. That rule is if your patio shares at least two of the following, it is included: the slab, a wall, and the roof. Otherwise it is part of your landscape. There are two areas of your backyard that are okay for the fire element. That is the fame/reputation area and the relationship area (preferably the fame/reputation area, because this sector is represented by the fire element). This area is located in the center back of your home or your yard. The grill is also okay in the relationship area, the back right corner, because fire renews and replenishes the earth. Hope that answers your question.

Happy Grilling!
~ Paul

Q. My husband and I moved into our home about a year ago. Our relationship isn't what it used to be. We don't share the closeness we used to or agree on much. It is almost like we just tolerate each other. Is there something we can do to Feng Shui our marriage?

Jen
Cedar Park, Texas

A. Well, let's start by looking at your bedroom and at your relationship area. First, wherever your bedroom is in your home, it needs to be a room that depicts the feeling you want in your relationship. If you want passion, put pictures of couples sharing the kind of passion you want to experience in your relationship. Sit down together and decide what you would like to share, and transform that room into that feel. Paint this room!! You want it to hold you as you spend time together! Second, you need to look at your actual relationship area of the home. You really don't want a child's room here, or they will come between you and your husband. Make sure this area holds things in two's, such as art or candles. Pictures of you two would also work well here. This should not be a spare bedroom. You want this area activated with your energy. Have fun and be creative and make this a project you work on together!

~ Blessings,
Leigh

Q. If I place a flowing water element in my lawn, which direction should it face?

Annette
Austin, Texas

A. Great question. One of the many attributes of water is its representation of abundance and good fortune. Facing the flow towards your door will help to direct chi to your home, bringing with it abundance and good fortune. The water element in your lawn will also attract life, such as birds and other animals, which is in fact bringing life force energy to your home. This combination will help to create a balance of earthly energy, material objects such as wealth, and spiritual energy, life itself, which in turn will energize the inhabitance of your home. Hope that answers your question.

~ Paul

Q. We are trying to sell our home with no luck. I heard that there are Feng Shui "cures" to put into place to help in the selling process. What are some things that might help?

Louis
Houston, Texas

A. Selling your home can be frustrating. Especially since we must continually try to keep it in tip-top shape for people to come through at any moment. The best place to start is to clear out the clutter so that you are only using what you need, and this makes keeping the home neat a much easier process. A few other ideas would be to locate the wealth area of the yard (back lefthand corner) and add the colors of purple and gold. This can be done with flowers (an ideal choice), ribbon or anything with those colors. This will activate that sector, bringing in more money for your home. Next, buy some plastic bunnies (don't spend a lot of money) and put them in the helpful people sector of the yard (front right). Because bunnies multiply so quickly, this will represent your helpful people multiplying in order to sell. Consider sprucing up the lawn, this will attract energy into your home and also attract a buyer. Sometimes that first impression is enough to make them see the potential in your home and they can see themselves living there!

Blessings,
Paul

To view more of our questions or ask your own, visit:

www.thefengshuitrainingcenter.com/studentlounge

Bibliography

Beckwith, M (2006) *The Secret (*DVD) Prime Time Productions

Boldt, L. (1999) *The Tao of Abundance.* Penguin USA

Byrne, R, (2006) *The Secret (*DVD) Prime Time Productions

Delorey, C. (2000) *Life Cycles, Your emotional journey to freedom and happiness.* Osmos books

Linn, D. (2000) *Space Clearing.* McGraw-Hill

Vitale, J, (2006) *The Secret (*DVD) Prime Time Productions

Ruiz, D. (1997) *The Four Agreements.* Amber-Allen Publishing, Inc.

About the Author

Leigh has been studying Feng Shui since 1999. She began her practice in 2004 and began teaching in 2006. Leigh is Co-Owner/Co-Director and instructor for The Feng Shui Training Center, with her husband Paul. She has written one book on Feng Shui, *Your Life, Designed*, and has started her second book about Feng Shui in the classroom. Leigh is a member of the International Feng Shui Guild and is a volunteer at the local elementary school, volunteering her time and her Feng Shui knowledge to improve the learning environment of both the teachers and students.

Leigh practices and teaches the BTB Sect of Feng Shui. Leigh was recently asked if the BTB Sect of Feng Shui was a cult. The answer is no! Feng Shui is not about religion, but about surrounding yourself with reminders of your goals. In other words, it is all about intention. Leigh has chosen the BTB style of Feng Shui because it is contemporary, practical, and resonates with her. All styles of Feng Shui are equally effective; the key is to find the one that resonates with you.

Leigh works with her clients to come up with unique cures, and limits the number of cookie cutter cures used in a consultation. She believes the more relevance the cure has for the client the better results they will see for themselves. Her style is to have the client take ownership in the creation process of their lives and enjoy the tremendous results of their efforts. Leigh makes Feng Shui easy, practical, and rewarding.

Leigh's newest project is a new series called Feng Shui Your Way, which can be viewed free on-demand at www.fengshuiyourway.tv and at www.onneteworks.com

www.ingramcontent.com/pod-product-compliance
Lightning Source LLC
LaVergne TN
LVHW051550070426
835507LV00021B/2514